WHAT PEOPLE ARE SA

HONEY IN THE RIVER

Marsha Scarbrough fell in love with a polygamous West African shaman and tells the tale in her smart, sexy memoir *Honey in the River*. Explicit, funny and above all erotic, Scarbrough questions monogamy, experiments with polygamy and embraces a little-known indigenous religion. In so doing she plunges the reader into a world of trance, rhythm and ancient African mythology. A remarkable tour de force of sexual and emotional healing.
Margaret Leslie Davis, bestselling author of *Dark Side of Fortune, Mona Lisa in Camelot*

Marsha Scarbrough's painfully honest writing at once reveals stark truths and privation and revels in glorious erotic excess as she relives the blazing arc of her relationship across race, cultural norms and conventions. This true story merges reality with myth, the body with the soul, and the sexual with the spiritual to powerful effect.
Neil Besner, author, literary critic, editor, Provost and Vice-President, Academic and International, The University of Winnipeg

When a woman tells the truth about her life, the veils between the worlds open so that true love can be revealed. Marsha Scarbrough kept my heart open to receive her story, page after page. This book is about the gift of self love.
Joanna Harcourt-Smith, author of *Tripping the Bardo* with Timothy Leary

Scarbrough shows us her scars. She bravely unwraps herself, offering us her history and her soul. We see the author for what she truly is: a beautiful human being, making light, seeking healing. *Honey in the River* helps us understand the complexities of social conditioning, and what can happen when we allow ourselves to experience and embrace both the human drama and universal mystery. Questions ensue.

Dr. Anya, Reiki Master, Relationship Coach, author of *Opening Love*

Marsha's book is a deeply heartfelt journey into love, shamanism and human mysteries. She warmly takes us as her passengers, to spiritual and moral destinations that we could not experience without her courage to explore and share.

Pen Densham, Writer/Producer/Director The Twilight Zone TV series, Outer Limits TV series, Robin Hood: Prince of Thieves

Honey in the River

Shadow, Sex and West African Spirituality

Honey in the River

Shadow, Sex and West African Spirituality

Marsha Scarbrough

CHANGE
MAKERS
BOOKS

Winchester, UK
Washington, USA

First published by Changemakers Books, 2015
Changemakers Books is an imprint of John Hunt Publishing Ltd., Laurel House, Station Approach,
Alresford, Hants, SO24 9JH, UK
office1@jhpbooks.net
www.johnhuntpublishing.com
www.changemakers-books.com

For distributor details and how to order please visit the 'Ordering' section on our website.

Text copyright: Marsha Scarbrough 2014
www.marshascarbrough.com

ISBN: 978 1 78279 948 1
Library of Congress Control Number: 2014958930

A CIP catalogue record for this book is available from the British Library.

Design: Stuart Davies

Printed and bound by CPI Group (UK) Ltd, Croydon, CR0 4YY, UK

We operate a distinctive and ethical publishing philosophy in all
areas of our business, from our global network of authors to
production and worldwide distribution.

CONTENTS

For Catherine Chabot Davis
Thank you for the creative sanctuary you so generously offered,
for you brilliant critiques, for your insightful editing. Thank
you for your support and encouragement, for being my chosen
sister/mother, for withholding judgment about my questionable
life choices. I miss your sharp intellect, your love of parties,
your ready laugh. I miss you.

Acknowledgements

Although writing is a solitary process, the loving support of friends and colleagues made this book possible. I'm deeply grateful to all who offered encouragement and insight as I followed a long and winding path to publication. I extend special thanks to Tim Ward, who has been my literary champion, fierce critic and caring friend. Thanks also to steadfast Jenny Sanborn, who read at least three drafts and suggested the perfect title. Lindsay Smith's brilliant analysis helped me spin the story in the right direction. Nina Sammons served as reassuring oracle. Dawn Wink brought her novelist's sensibilities, offered practical suggestions and pumped up my strength for the home stretch. Margaret Leslie Davis shared her signature moxie by offering unflagging inspiration. Thank you, John Hunt, for believing in me, twice! Warm appreciation to everyone at John Hunt Publishing for doing the work it takes to transform a dream into reality. Finally, I acknowledge Oba for providing this powerful material.

The people you love,
you know like
the touch of their fingertips.
The people who love you,
you will never know.
Yoruba song as translated by Oba

Prologue

Oshun is in love with Shango, but he's married to Oya. Oshun thinks Shango will leave his wife and choose her if she can cook the foods he loves. She asks Oya to share her recipe for Shango's favorite soup. Oya suspects that Oshun is sleeping with her husband, and Oya wants revenge. She tells Oshun, "If you want your man to love you as much as Shango loves me, you have to put some of your body in the soup, like your ear. The sweetness will keep him from knowing what he's eating." Oshun is a bad cook anyway. She cuts off her whole ear and throws it in the soup. When she serves the soup to Shango, he sees something floating on top of the soup and asks, "Oshun, what's this?" Oshun says, "Oya told me to put it in because you would like it. It's my ear." Shango doesn't like the ear soup. He blames his wife for tricking his lover into disfiguring herself, so he divorces Oya and marries Oshun. That's why Oshun and Oya hate each other, and Oshun always wears a headwrap to cover her missing ear. The Yoruba people of West Africa tell this story. In their spiritual tradition, known as Ifa, Oshun, Oya and Shango are divinities called *orishas*, who serve as intermediaries between humans and the ultimate creator. *Orishas* also represent the archetypal energies which compose human complexity. The mythology of Ifa dramatizes the primal conflicts of our lives. Oshun represents love and eroticism. Shango represents anger, aggressive sexuality and justice. Oya is truth.

I am one of many women who have made this soup. It's a sticky soup with a bitter aftertaste, and we often add more enticing body parts than just our ears. Cleaning up the mess can take most of a lifetime.

Honey in the River tells the story of my experiences with one Yoruba priest (called a *babalawo*). I don't know if he is representative of other Yoruba spiritual leaders. I'm simply an observer of Ifa practices and a participant in many ceremonies, not an

1

initiate nor an anthropologist. My reporting is subjective. From my point of view, this story is completely true, although I can't vouch for the reliability of my informants. I've changed names and details to protect privacy, but all these events happened. The other characters might recount the same events differently. In some of those stories, I would be cast as the villain. Those versions might also be true.

My encounter with this unfamiliar religion caused me to question my basic assumptions about monogamy, love, life and death. My story is both archetypal drama and epic soap opera. Blood is spilled. Friends are betrayed. Lovers are deceived. Some readers may be shocked at my behavior, dislike me or question my sanity. Others may think I was naïve, immoral, judgmental or just plain stupid. Please read on. I'll take you for a wild ride through sexual passion, secrecy, jealousy, anger and tragedy. I'll put aside my fears about what you may think of me to tell my uncensored truth. I'll take off my headwrap and show you the messy scars around my metaphorical missing ear.

Chapter 1

Possessed

2008

His blue-black skin contrasted sharply with the white sheets of his hospital bed. He was unconscious. A respirator controlled his breathing. Bandages swathed one arm. His upper lip was split and bloody. Wires connected him to beeping, blinking monitors. He was surrounded by his four wives, all middle-aged white American women, in shock, united by crisis, still wary of each other.

I was one of those wives.

June 1996

Cold water rushed around my ankles and over my pale, bare feet. Dressed in a pure white skirt and blouse, with a white scarf wrapping my blond curls, I stood in a clear canyon stream. Yellow rose petals filled my cupped hands. I prayed to Oshun by scattering these petals on the fresh water and watching them float away towards the sea. Oshun rules love, beauty and eroticism. She is the river. She is the flowing fresh water that caressed my feet. Other women and men, also dressed in white, waded beside me.

Golden objects glittered in the sun on the nearby shore. Oshun loves gold. Her favorite color is yellow, so we honored her with an altar of yellow cloth laden with yellow fruit, yellow candies, golden necklaces, a gilded bowl of yellow rose petals and a mirror, so she could admire her beautiful self. Her signature peacock feathers spilled from a brass vase and bobbed in the breeze. Honey is her favorite offering. We took turns drizzling it into the river.

As we washed our hands, faces and feet, a rich, deep voice

sang her name, *"Eh-way dah Oshun."*[1] Our *babalawo*, the leader of this ceremony, chanted praises to this *orisha* in a syncopated, flowing rhythm that mimicked the swirling currents of the river. He sang in Yoruba, his tonal native language. The words meant, "Look at beauty, look at Oshun." My hips swayed to the lyrical song.

Soon drums joined his chant. The rhythm became ever more sensuous and visceral. Our bodies danced. Hips, shoulders and arms swung in unending circles. I leaned forward, placed my hands on the outside of my thighs and moved them up over my hips, waist and breasts as I straightened up, as though smoothing sweet amber honey on my body. I feigned looking in a hand mirror to admire my hair and lips. I pushed my pelvis forward provocatively, then swung my hips back to display my gently bouncing booty. The song repeated. The dancers improvised and undulated responding to the vibration of drum and voice. We entered a non-verbal dialogue with the drummers, speaking directly soul-to-soul.

As sound and movement continued, dancers and drummers fell into deep trance. I lost all sense of time and place. My body danced with no effort or thought. Energy of pure eroticism moved from the water into my feet, up my legs, into my pelvis, through my abdomen, to my heart, out my arms, up my neck and into my empty brain. I became Oshun. She possessed me. I no longer existed, but Oshun was alive. My rational, cautious, sensible self disappeared. Through the dance, I became reckless lust personified. When the music finally stopped, my body sank to the earth beside other dancers. Gradually, Oshun left me. I found my way back into my skin and rested in afterglow. I'd experienced ancient African magic, but I was not in Africa. I was in Topanga Canyon, just north of the sprawling metropolis of Los Angeles.

Were we practicing voodoo? No, "voodoo" is a pejorative misnomer for a sophisticated system of spirituality born and practiced in West Africa for thousands of years before Christian missionaries arrived. We were practicing Ifa, the indigenous religion of the Yoruba people of what is now Nigeria. It is not black magic. In fact, it is not magic at all. Ifa practitioners are clear that what they do is a focused spiritual practice that creates healing for individuals and communities through the positive vibrations of drumming, dancing and chanting affirmations. In my experience, this practice is entirely joyful and life-affirming. Can Ifa be misused? Perhaps, but Ifa's shadowy reputation (as well as that of its sister religions Vodou in Haiti, Santeria in Cuba, Umbanda and Candomble in Brazil) probably resulted from fear felt by slave owners in the Americas when they observed the power of ceremonies without explanation of the intention behind the process. You'd be scared too if physically strong African slaves (who had good reasons to hate white people) were dancing around a fire in your backyard, in deep trance, chanting in a language you didn't understand. Such ceremonies were outlawed. Drums were destroyed. Native languages were forbidden. The religion was labeled as evil black magic by people who made no attempt to understand it.

Likewise, the first missionaries who ventured into Africa must have projected their fear onto the practices. They saw evil devil worship in a philosophy that did not even include the idea of evil or the concept of a devil. Perhaps giving "voodoo" a bad rap was an intentional tactic designed to help oppress powerful cultures. As with Native Americans, separating indigenous African people from their traditional spirituality was an effective technique for controlling them.

Why did Ifa interest me, a college-educated 49-year-old white woman with a career in film production? I am a seeker. Since the death of my parents and the end of my 18-year marriage, I'd spent 10 years exploring unconventional spiritual paths. I studied Buddhism. I trained in martial arts. I delved into dance therapy. I studied healing with a Native American medicine man

5

whose primary techniques involved drumming, dancing and chanting. When I discovered Ifa, I recognized the basic metaphysics of sacred vibration and reverence for the earth coupled with a rich mythology. My curiosity was triggered. A philosophy deeply rooted in the pre-Christian past hinted at universal truths that preceded the divisions of organized religions. I was always seeking the next level of spiritual experience, and Ifa promised to take me there.

My knowledge of this exotic worldview came from one teacher, Oba Odumade, a *babalawo* from Nigeria. Oba was a traditional healer and diviner as well as a master drummer and ceremonial leader. As he sang the chant to Oshun, Oba dazzled in the bright California sun. His midnight-black skin glistened with a sheen of sweat earned from his energetic drumming and singing. The breeze playfully buffeted his billowing white robe emblazoned with golden embroidery. Dark locks dangled below a jaunty cap that covered the bald crown of his head. His big presence belied his average height, and he looked two decades younger than his 55 years. He was not particularly handsome with a broad nose, thick lips and a slightly pug visage, but when his brilliant smile blazed across his face, he was the most beautiful man alive. Sparkling ivory teeth contrasted with sweet chocolate skin. He bestowed that smile like a prize on those who pleased him.

In ceremony, Oba pumped positive energy. His voice, rich, deep and velvety in conversation, could fly to falsetto and drop to booming bass in the course of one song. He strutted with his chalice-shaped *djembe* drum between his legs. He glided like a swan as he beat the barrel-shaped *djun djun* drum. He bobbed and wiggled his ass as he danced. He could sing, dance and drum all at once. His stage presence riveted us, and he thoroughly enjoyed the spotlight. He exuded love toward all the celebrants, and we fell in love with the song of his spirit over and over again. When he threw his head back in an open-throated laugh, my heart melted. To me, he was a natural man, bubbling with joy and fully alive. His positive masculinity was unencumbered by the macho posturing, disconnected intellect and controlling ego I saw in the men of my own culture. Oba lived in the moment. Whoever or whatever he focused on had his full attention. When he focused on me, I shined in the warm light of his eyes.

1992

I met Oba in May 1992. Los Angeles was on fire. A jury acquitted four white police officers of beating African-American Rodney King. It was ridiculous. Everyone saw the videotape of the defenseless and outnumbered King being viciously struck with nightsticks. It was a brutal example of excessive force. When the verdict was announced, the city went crazy. Not the whole city, fires blazed in the African-American neighborhoods of South Central and Watts. Vandalism, looting and rampant destruction moved north toward downtown. Curfew was instituted. Fear blanketed my hometown. I felt an undeniable mandate for healing.

Los Angeles was MY city. I was born in Queen of Angels hospital beside the Hollywood Freeway. I grew up in working-class Latino neighborhoods. I excelled at academics in public high school and won scholarships to USC, where I lived on a rich white island in black South Central. This wasn't the first African-American uprising. In August 1965, during summer vacation between my freshman and sophomore years, police brutality triggered the Watts Riots which left 34 dead, over 1,000 people injured and $40 million in property damage. Proximity to the campus motivated the USC administration to send a reassuring letter to parents before classes resumed. When I returned to campus, I was horrified at my classmates' inherent racism, with one fraternity brazenly flying a Confederate flag.

In my last year of school, I fell in love with a sexy Chicano artist and married him after graduation. My parents did not approve and disowned me for crossing a racial line. I found a new family among the artists and bohemians of Echo Park, Silverlake and Mt. Washington. During and after college, I worked in an advertising office in densely urban downtown and studied martial arts with a Japanese master in Glendale. After a decade, I broke into the entertainment industry and worked as an assistant director on major feature films and prime time television. I found a new home in the studios and backlots of Hollywood, West L.A. and the San Fernando Valley. I worked with celebrities, like Mary Tyler Moore, Leonard Nimoy, Pierce Brosnan, and Clint Eastwood. I was especially impressed with Eastwood's mastery of craft as a director and admired his cool grace under fire. My parents died. My marriage ended. I began to study Native American spirituality, and I found another home in sweatlodges hidden in quiet backyards throughout the city.

Los Angeles was a magical place for me. From the wilds of the Hollywood Hills to the weirdness of Venice, the city embraced diversity in its cuisines, architecture, philosophies, arts and ethnic communities. Not only did it flaunt Chinatown, it boasted Little Tokyo, Little Armenia, Thaitown and Little Ethiopia. Fairfax was more than a street. It was the heart of Jewish culture. To me, this vibrant mix of mankind was the true beauty of my city of angels. Seeing it go up in flames broke my heart. I, personally, needed to do something about it.

As I drove on a freeway flanked by Beltane fires fueled by centuries of interracial anger, my thoughts wandered from this injustice toward African-Americans to the injustice suffered by Native Americans and how reconnecting with indigenous spirituality was helping to heal their rage around genocide. Native American spiritual practices were outlawed at conquest. Without that anchor, the people were lost and easy to dismiss. Self-esteem was shattered. Now sweatlodges and Sun Dances are bringing Native people back to themselves, to personal power. Healing is in process. It occurred to me that Africans have an indigenous spirituality too. It also has been denigrated and outlawed, labeled "voodoo." I wondered what wisdom could be found in this original ancient religion and how it could be retrieved. Perhaps racism in America could be healed if African-Americans reconnected with their spiritual roots. On the radio, Rodney King asked, "Can we all get along?" I answered, "Yes!" I vowed that bringing the races together in harmony would be my quest.

Within the week, I got a mailer about a workshop in West African shamanism presented by Oba Odumade, who had just arrived in Los Angeles. It said drums would be provided, but we were to bring fruit for the ceremony. I signed up, curious about what we'd do with the fruit.

On a Saturday morning, I showed up with a bag of bananas and oranges. About 20 pale-skinned people were milling around, no African-Americans in attendance. I didn't know anyone, but it was clear that I was one of many white folks seeking the deeper truths of indigenous cultures. Drums of different sizes and shapes were everywhere. Some were big cylinders with skin stretched over both ends. Some were chalice-shaped with a skin over the rim. Some were tapering cylinders with skin on the wide end. Chairs were set up in a circle. I figured out I was supposed to select a drum that spoke to me, take it to one of the chairs in the circle and wait.

Finally, Oba Odumade swept into the room on a cloud of colorful, flowing robes. His dark skin glowed with vibrant energy. His electric smile lit up the room. He oozed charisma as he welcomed us in a thick accent blending British with the melody of his native tongue.

The morning was devoted to teaching us basic drumming, and I was completely lost. Various hand positions produced different sounds. Rhythms were constantly shifting. I didn't have the manual dexterity or the ear to keep up, although some people were already accomplished drummers. Oba flipped through charts that seem to be splattered with single syllables: *gun, go, pa.*

Are those words? Everything I tried to play was wrong. I felt frustrated.

Oba was clearly a drum virtuoso. He pounded out complex rhythms at lightning speed while beaming pure joy. His drum seemed to be part of him. He played easily and naturally, as though he entered a trance and disappeared into his music. He was relaxed and playful teaching a task I found overwhelming and incomprehensible.

In the afternoon, he gathered our fruit and assembled it into an artistic altar, a concretization of abundance. As drums pounded, little bowls of salt, honey and sugar were passed around. Oba sang in his African language. His compelling voice moved me. I couldn't follow the intricacies of the ceremony, but I danced. At the end, we ate the fruit.

Dazzled and confused by my first glimpse of this exotic new world, little did I know that, as with Eve, those few bites of fruit would completely change my life.

Oba's wife, Miriam, assisted him. A Jewish woman in her early 40s, she was *zaftig* with frizzy dyed hair showing gray roots and an earthy, Old Testament presence. She also had a loud voice with a harsh Bronx accent which was a startling contrast to her African attire. At the end of the day, I thanked Miriam and asked her if I could set up an interview with Oba as research for a screenplay I was writing about Peace Corps volunteers in Africa. She snapped, "You'd have to pay him to do that." Her aggressive New York style took me by surprise and put me off. Since my screenplay was a spec script, paying for an interview was out of the question.

At that moment of my life, I'd been divorced for five years. I was 45 years old and lonely. I felt like I'd failed at love and was unlovable. Yet I saw this exotic, interesting, sexy man with an abrasive, unappealing woman. I wondered, *If she can get a man like that, why can't I?*

1993

A year later, my path unexpectedly led me back to Ifa. My friend Mark, a bearded, shaggy-haired Episcopal priest who wore Birkenstocks and bracelets, invited me to help him plan a 24-hour healing vigil for Los Angeles to be held on the first anniversary of the uprising. Twenty-four different spiritual groups from the many cultures of Los Angeles (including Native Americans, Korean Buddhists, Catholics, Hindus, Buddhists of African Descent and Baha'is) would each take an hour to perform ceremony, prayer, meditation, sacred music or dance to heal the racial tensions of the city. I decided to produce and direct a *pro bono* documentary about the event. Those were the days before video could be shot on cellphones, so I recruited volunteers with video cameras to take shifts shooting the event. If I was lucky enough to have more than one camera at a time, I would make sure each camera was shooting from a different angle. I planned to stay up all night and oversee everything.

Several hours into the vigil, Oba Odumade appeared beaming with joy, draped in an elegant white robe, topped with a sparkling silver-sequined hat. An entourage of drummers and dancers followed him, Miriam was among them, but she faded into the background as he performed. He immediately raised the energy in the room. In his commanding voice, he called in the ancestors and the spirits of the earth to heal the city.

"This is a special ceremony. This ceremony is for all mankind."

He pointed to the black skin of his arm and continued, "This is just a dress we put on. In the face of Obatala, in the face of Ifa, in the face of Shango, in the face of Yemoja, this is our dress. The solution that faces mankind, only God has it."

After hours of quiet meditations and gentle prayers, I knew this footage would be dynamite. I was blessed to have three cameras rolling.

He led the crowd in a playful chanting of vowels.

"Uh-hummm, aahhh, ah-ha! Now I see! That's all! That's what life is! Leave everything in the hands of the Almighty Creator, whoever you believe in, focus your mind there."

Then he took the rest of his hour and totally rocked the house with high-energy joy. Drumming! Singing! Dancing! We all jumped to our feet and shook our bodies to the wild beat.

"How are you feeling?" he asked.

"Good!" we responded in unison.

He threw his head back in pure lovely laughter. During one call-and-response song that he translated as "Something good is happening, he directed the call to me. I sang the response, "I can feel it!"—and sparks flew between us in an instant, electric moment of connection.

Since Oba's hour of ceremony was shot with three cameras, I had three hours of footage to edit into a few minutes of screen time. I needed Oba to review the footage with me and help create a concise narration. I called, hoping I wouldn't be thwarted by his fierce gatekeeper, but this time Miriam was cooperative.

As we screened the footage, Oba emphasized that Ifa is "a focused spiritual practice. It's not magic. It's an ancient technology for healing people and communities." He explained that this technology heals through a complex combination of vibration, psychological archetypes, herbal remedies and identification with the primal energies of Nature.

"In my tradition, drumming, dancing and chanting are forms of prayer. The rhythms I play and teach are sacred vibrations coded to create healing."

As Oba translated the lyrics of the chants, I recognized affirmations of positive outcomes: "I am alive and well!" and "Something good is happening!"

I resonated with this concept immediately because it's precisely what I learned from my Native American teacher. I'd been studying with Archer, a Sioux shaman also known as John Gonzalez, since shortly after my divorce. He'd guided me through many sweatlodges and marathon dances in the past five years. I'd embraced his explanation of indigenous metaphysics. He believed that vibration can heal us because we are composed of constantly moving energy. As quantum physics confirms, matter (including us) is simply electrons vibrating at various rates. Indigenous wisdom recognizes that positive vibrations (certain rhythms, repetitive movement, chants) can realign energy that has fallen out of harmony.

"Ifa addresses the complexity of human psychology with a specific belief system," Oba continued.

"In this mythology, Oludumare is the energy of creation, perhaps equivalent to the western idea of God. Oludumare is the intelligence above all. It's not a being. It's simply energy. Before people and animals come to live on Earth, they have to answer to Oludumare about what they want to do here. So when difficult things happen, we can't ask why. We must just accept."

I recalled Archer's parable that before we come to Earth, we decide exactly what is going to happen to us so that we can learn the lessons we want to learn in this life. When we are born, we forget what we've agreed to and spend our lives trying to remember to learn the lessons.

"Oludumare presides over the *orishas*, who are intermediaries between humans and Oludumare," Oba elaborated.

"*Orishas* are actual historic persons who have ascended to divine status after their deaths in the distant past, like Catholic saints, but each *orisha* also embodies universal energy that is identified with a natural element. For example, Oshun, the *orisha* who represents the energy of love and eroticism, is a beautiful woman, but she is also the river."

This was new information for me. I was intrigued, but I recognized that this philosophy was far too complex to explain in a snippet of this documentary. I asked Oba to keep it simple for now.

"Of course," he smiled, "but you should understand that

when we dance, we enter a trance. When we are in that state, one of the *orishas* may merge its energy with ours and ride us. In a sense, dancers can become possessed."

Oba was intelligent, quick and charming. I told him I'd like to learn more about Ifa. He explained that learning dance, drumming and the religion all go together and invited me to take his drumming and dance classes. I jumped at the chance. Although my introduction to Ifa was minimal, I sensed that it held deep truths for me. Oba was the real thing. He was a natural man from outside conventional western culture. He could teach the wisdom of Nature, of our senses, of our bodies. I hungered for ancient healing that went beyond my mind to my sensual, kinetic core. Ifa, and Oba, implicitly promised it.

During their first year in Los Angeles, Oba and Miriam established Ifa Center, a space for teaching and a home for their spiritual community. It was housed in a commercial rental. On the street level, raw warehouse space surrounded an open-air courtyard. Living quarters for Oba, Miriam and their seven-year-old son David filled the second floor. The location, an ethnically-diverse section of Los Angeles still just flirting with gentrification, was ideal for building their multi-racial, spiritual community. Although other tribal drumming groups existed in Los Angeles, Ifa Center was unique in that it taught indigenous African culture to a rainbow of people. Its spiritual intention and multi-racial congregation made it different from drum circles in Venice, Topanga Canyon or Leimert Park. During Saturday morning drumming and dance classes, the space felt industrial and utilitarian, but at night, flickering candlelight and mesmerizing rhythm transformed it into a magical dreamscape.

Oba celebrated every full moon and new moon with a community ceremony. For these evening celebrations, he created sacred space by hanging colorful fabric over gray cinderblock walls. He built mysterious altars in dark corners. He lit the night with candles and oil lamps, and smudged with sage and frankincense, leaving the air thick with fragrant smoke. Celebrants arrived dressed in ethnic splendor. Drum-toting men wore loose shirts of African textiles. Women wore sparkling jewelry with flowing fabrics of eclectic origins. Oba made a grand entrance with his smile blazing and laughter twinkling in his eyes. As he moved among the people, robes in brilliant hues of bright blue, rich maroon or acid green fluttered around him. Strings of glass beads hung like garlands around his neck, and an embroidered hat topped his head. He sang out to call in Spirit, "*Ajaja!*"[2] We responded, "*A mee lo!*" The drumming began. Intensity escalated. Tempo quickened. Each dancer responded to the beat in a unique way. Shoulders shimmied. Arms waved. Heads bobbed. Hips swayed. Trance enveloped everyone.

Soon dancers and drummers engaged in sacred conversations without words. Dancers listened to the messages of drummers. Drummers watched the bodies of dancers. Each responded to and influenced the other. As in making love, individual energies merged into transcendent communion. We throbbed together for hours.

Oba had stamina. He sang and drummed for about three hours without a break. Then he rested for about half an hour, ate some fruit or drank a Guinness, then played for another three hours. We matched his energy. The rhythm kept us going far beyond exhaustion.

The throbbing bodies were a mix of different colors, ages, sizes and styles. Each had a different reason for being there. Asante, an African-American woman from Texas, had reinvented herself as glittering black royalty, bedecked with golden jewelry, flowing shawls and mighty locks. For ceremony, she dressed in gossamer white with her ample black midriff exposed. She proudly flaunted stretch marks as the trophies of childbirth. Asante was often accompanied by Guy, a slender, soft-spoken Frenchman who obviously adored her. Bernadette, a sexy 30ish Latina, favored short skirts and low necklines. She stayed close to Oba and flirted with him openly. I met Mildred, a retired psychotherapist in her 70s, in a dance therapy group. Although she looked like a typical little old lady from the Midwest, she was a wild woman interested in every type of mind-body therapy. She danced along with the best of us. Manuel, a mature, accomplished drummer with bushy gray hair worked as a sound editor on major feature films. Sidney, a tall, thin, blonde feminist, was an accomplished screenwriter and my close friend. Although we both worked in the show-business world, our friendship grew in goddess workshops and Jungian dream circles. Sidney, Asante and I knew each other in another context as well. In the aftermath of the uprising, we'd all joined a women's sweatlodge group in South Central. We met monthly for spiritual connection. Of eight women in the circle, only Sidney and I were not of African descent.

Many of the participants were attractive young women and men, but older people, like me, Sidney, Asante, Manuel and Mildred were a strong presence. An elderly African-American man, who walked with a cane, was an honored regular. Many of the drummers were young men with long hair or blond dreadlocks, who vied for Oba's time and attention. Some nearly worshiped him with "bromance" in their eyes. As much as we wanted to learn to drum, explore Ifa or experience being possessed by *orishas*, Oba's presence was what drew us in.

Despite differences, everyone was sincerely seeking something: love, joy, community, spiritual growth. Combining elements of tribal rituals, hippie love-ins and raves, the ceremonies were intoxicating, uplifting and utterly fun. In practice, Ifa is a sexy, physical religion. Late in the ceremony, when the drumming got hot, dancers crowded the floor and candles created a mysterious half-light, Oba played Yankay, a hypnotic rhythm and chant that translates as "cast it out." As the rhythm took the dancers, they spontaneously fell backwards into the crowd, trusting that they would be caught, and they were.

They fell on "Yan" and were tossed back to their feet on "Kay." Healing comes from the embodied knowledge that your community has your back and helps you get back on your feet.

At these bi-monthly ceremonies, in fact at all of Oba's ceremonies, healing was evident. The elder who hobbled in leaning on a cane sometimes left it behind when he headed home. A woman slumped in a wheelchair reached for a rattle, shook it to the rhythm, then to her own surprise, stood up and shimmied from head to toe. My own exhilaration lasted for days.

Although Ifa Center tended to be disorganized, the practice itself, as taught by Oba, was authentic, invigorating and demanding. Oba said, "Drumming is advanced meditation because you cannot think and drum at the same time." In drumming class, he explained that the drum is a sacred altar.

"A tree and an animal died to make it, and we bring them alive again with our energy." He told us we all have a drum within us: our heart.

"Our heart is our battery, and the drum is its charger."

Oba suggested I learn to play the *djembe*, a chalice-shaped wooden shell with a goatskin head. *Djembe* is played with the hands. The sacred rhythms are actual songs composed of three specific notes in an endless variety of combinations. The language of the drum for *djembe* is *gun, go do* and *pa ta*, the mysterious code of the flip chart I found so confusing in the first workshop. *Gun* is the bass note, played with an open palm in the center of the drumhead. *Go* is the intermediate tone, played with the fingers only as the knuckles at the top of the palm rest on the rim. *Pa* is the high note, played as a slap of the fingertips on the drumhead with the heel of the hand resting on the rim.

This language and teaching technique was introduced in America by Babatunde Olatunji, the Nigerian drummer known for his groundbreaking 1959 album *Drums of Passion* and his collaborations with Carlos Santana and The Grateful Dead. Oba performed and traveled with Olatunji for over 10 years.

I preferred dancing to drumming, but Oba required us to learn basic drumming before he allowed us to join dance class. He insisted that we must be able to distinguish the three notes and know basic rhythm patterns to have the acute listening required of dancers. Once I started dancing, I didn't catch on to things quickly. I could tell Oba felt frustrated with me when I didn't start on the correct beat. I felt like crying, partly from wanting to please him, partly for just feeling like a failure. Later he told me he enjoyed having me in class. I laughed and said, "But I'm terrible."

"No, you're not. You just need to relax your mind."

I came back week after week and made slow progress.

As I learned more about drumming and dance, I learned more about the *orishas* because each *orisha* has specific songs, rhythms and dances. Each *orisha* also has particular colors and favorite offerings. Like gods and goddesses in the ancient Greek pantheon, the *orishas'* relationships to each other reflect complex human behaviors including love, lust, anger, violence, adultery and betrayal. Oba claims the Greeks stole their mythology from the Yorubas. The similarities are striking. Oshun is the equivalent of Aphrodite. Like Hermes, Eshu plays tricks and serves as messenger to the other divinities. Yemoja/Olokun rules the seas like Poseidon. Shango throws thunderbolts and exacts justice like Zeus.

As I got to know the major *orishas*, I recognized that they were archetypes. Carl Jung, the founder of analytical psychology, noticed that certain images, symbols and concepts (such as the great mother, the wise old man or the trickster) appear cross-culturally from ancient times to the present. He speculated that these archetypes arise from the collective unconscious and speak to us through our individual dreams and our communal mythologies. Jung wrote that the number of archetypes is limitless. Oba tells us that in Ifa there are at least 400 orishas, maybe more.

Oba was clear that the *orishas* are metaphors for different aspects of human nature, yet *orishas* are also actual elements of our natural world (such as the river, fire or the ocean). Oba taught that we all have all the *orishas* within us and Ifa ceremonies allow us to experience their different energies. Similarly, Jung believed archetypes considered together reveal the complexity of the human psyche and experiential encounters with archetypal energies allow us to understand the divine nature of their wisdom.

"*Ori* means head, mind or consciousness, and, *Asha* means culture or character. Those words combine in *orisha*," Oba explained. "Usually one *orisha* rules each person. We call that dominant spiritual energy or personality characteristic our 'head.' We use ceremonies and offerings to invoke other *orisha* energies to balance our personality and improve our relationships with others."

According to Oba, each *orisha* is a channel of energy, and ceremony tunes us in to those channels. I speculated that Jung would approve of Ifa technology.

Eshu/Elegba

Oba introduced us to the *orishas* through ceremonies in their honor. The first such celebration at Ifa Center was for the trickster, Eshu, also known as Elegba. We dressed in white and brought offerings of red wine, cigars or hot peppers. We arrived after dark. Low light created mysterious shadows. Red and black fabric draped the walls. In one corner, candles illuminated a child-sized effigy with goat horns and hooves, standing on two feet, playfully brandishing a scepter topped with an erect phallus. Oba appeared in his white ceremonial robes accented by strands of red and black beads. He wore a peaked cap with sharply-pointed flaps extending from each side. This "dog-ear hat" heightens the wearer's intuition, allowing him to hear what humans cannot hear, to sense what's hidden. The hat looked ridiculous, but Oba wore it with such natural confidence that it became a badge of power.

"This is Eshu, the trickster. He lives behind our head and pushes us to make mistakes. He whispers in our ear to get us to make bad choices. When we acknowledge him, he will come out in front of our face where we can see him and honor him. Then he becomes the messenger to all the other *orishas*, so we always honor him first in every ceremony. Missionaries in Africa thought he was the devil because of his red and black colors, goat horns and hooves, but we Yoruba don't have the concept of the devil. He is our shadow. When we call him Elegba, he is the community's shadow. Elegba likes to start arguments and create conflict between people. Eshu makes his home at the crossroads, so he oversees our life choices. His companion is the vulture. He likes cigars, wine, whisky, chili and alligator pepper. He uses the shepherd's crooked stick to keep us in line."

Oba instructed us to lay our offerings at the effigy's feet as he chanted the invocation, *"Eshu shiwa ju"*[3] which translates as "go in front, don't go behind me." We formed a circle as the drums kicked in and the song shifted to our request, "do not influence me, do not push me." Oba demonstrated the dance by stomping one foot and shaking a fist (perhaps clutching an imaginary shepherd's crook) into the center of the circle, then stomping the other foot and shaking the other fist to the outside of the circle. The circle turned as we stomped and shook. The tempo sped up. We stomped and shook faster and faster, until the circle dissolved into wild free dancing. Eshu possessed dancers and pushed them into provocative moves. Ultimately, inhibitions dissolved and playful dirty dancing ruled the night. I bumped butts with Asante and shimmied my shoulders to bounce my breasts.

As the energy cooled down and the celebrants started to depart, Oba warned us.

"Don't be surprised if you see some changes in your life that you don't like. You've called Eshu out. Now he will show you your shadow. You may discover dark truths about yourself."

I stopped in my tracks and wondered, What am I in for? Is there yet another painful lesson I need to learn? I knew Eshu well. He's Jung's shadow archetype, our repressed instincts, weaknesses, addictions and secret shortcomings. I thought about all the shadow work I'd done: Jungian dream groups, psychotherapy, Native American fasting dances from sunset to sunrise. Surely, I'd befriended my shadow by now. What could Eshu have in store for me?

Ifa doesn't offer sweetness and light, unicorns and rainbows. It gives us an opportunity to take a good look at what we hide from the world, to learn from our transgressing behaviors. If we can face the truth and find the courage to change, our darkness becomes our connection to the divine.

At that moment, Eshu was a slightly unsettling concept. Later, he would tear my life to shreds.

Oba told us he was born in southwestern Nigeria to a Yoruba royal family. "*Oba*" means "king." "*Odumade*" means "scripture to be worshipped." The Yoruba are one of the largest ethnic groups in West Africa, estimated at 30 to 50 million people. Their origins may go back to the 4th century BC. Oba claimed that, "In the time of Moses, the Yoruba were slaves in Egypt who were freed at the same time as the Hebrews. While the Hebrews wandered, the Yoruba went straight to what is now western Nigeria and established their civilization." Their culture thrived between 1100 and 1900 AD and was known for fine bronze sculpture, pottery, textiles and music. According to Oba, the village where he was born was known for its sorcerers. His family moved to Lagos, the capital, when he was a child.

Some of the stories Oba told about his childhood disturbed me.

"I didn't like school, so I'd run away and go to the beach. When my mother found out, she chained me up at home."

With pain that still seemed fresh, he recounted being falsely accused of stealing a hymnal from church. His mother punished him by holding his hand on a hot griddle and was anguished when the book later turned up in another boy's possession.

"When I disobeyed her, she'd cut my skin and rub hot pepper into the wounds."

To me, these parenting practices were child abuse. I wanted to comfort this wounded little boy.

As a child, Oba was a musical prodigy. His father was a Christian church choirmaster, so Oba attended choir rehearsals and effortlessly learned to sing all the parts. When he showed interest in drumming, his family disapproved because members of the royal family are not supposed to be entertainers, but he showed such promise and interest that they relented. During the 1960s and early '70s (a time of cultural renaissance in Nigeria), he worked as a teacher during the day and played in clubs at night. He jammed at Nigerian Afrobeat musician Fela Kuti's famous compound and played as a session musician at Ginger Baker's Lagos studio. During these years, he had three illegitimate daughters by three different women.

The *orishas* chose Oba to be a *babalawo* when he was a teenager. His family never saw Ifa as a conflict with Christianity (although it was never discussed in church). Oba began training in herbalism, divination, Ifa liturgy, ceremony and music in his teens. Training continued until he was fully initiated in his 30s.

In the early 1980s, when his third daughter was only months old, Oba toured America with a band of Nigerian musicians, playing big shows in all the major cities of the eastern seaboard.

"On the last day of the tour, the promoter disappeared without paying us or returning our passports and plane tickets. We were stranded in Brooklyn. At first, we played in a nightclub and slept there when it was closed. Someone at the club told us to go to Central Park and talk to the African drummers there. We did, and one of those drummers took me to meet Baba Olatunji."

Olatunji took Oba in immediately, made him a member of his

band, gave him work and a place to live. Oba met Miriam, and soon she was pregnant. David was born. Oba's siblings were determined that this time he would get married. The oldest sister was sent to New York with a wedding dress for Miriam. Oba never returned to Nigeria. He toured with Olatunji playing huge venues as the opening act for The Grateful Dead and Carlos Santana. When Olatunji's schedule slowed, and he no longer needed Oba full time, Oba and Miriam moved to Los Angeles.

Obatala

On the night of the ceremony for the wise old man, Obatala, the walls of Ifa Center were draped in pure white. We dressed in white, wrapped our heads in white scarves and brought offerings of white flowers and white candles. An altar draped in white cloth was set with a simple glass of water and a white candle. Oba appeared in his white robes, with white beads and a white cap. Miriam, dressed in white with her head wrapped, made opening remarks.

"Thank you all for coming. The purpose of our gathering together for this ceremony is to create peace and harmony in our community." She deferred to Oba.

"Obatala is the *orisha* of creation and creativity because he made the land, then he made the people out of clay. He's represented as a white-bearded old man with a walking stick. His color is pure white."

Miriam excused herself to answer a knock at the door. As Oba began marking each of our foreheads with white chalk, we heard Miriam screaming from the other room, "How dare you! You are so disrespectful! Shame on you!" Peace and harmony evaporated in an instant. Miriam stormed upstairs. She'd gone ballistic because two celebrants showed up late in white shirts and blue jeans, instead of the requested pure white. They joined the circle sheepishly. Oba welcomed them warmly and marked their foreheads with white chalk. He chanted the invocation to Eshu (always the first prayer of any ceremony) then asked us to face north as he chanted Obatala's song, Ile Bobo, Ile Orisha.[4] We all faced south as he sang it again. We faced east and finally west. He translated the chant as, "The land belongs to Obatala because he made it."

After we placed our white flowers and candles on the altar, Oba joyfully called out "*Ajaja!?*" which asks, "Are there any spirits here?" We responded, "*A mee lo!*" answering, "I am here. I am Spirit!" The drums pounded in unison, then broke into syncopated rhythm. Dancers who'd been taking Oba's class entered, stepping in unison, each holding a six-foot bamboo walking stick, symbol of Obatala. Their sticks struck the earth simultaneously as they marched into a circle. Once in a circle, they started fancy choreography, leaping as they held their sticks skyward, shaking their sticks as they hopped, turning the sticks horizontally to create a square that finally morphed into a spinning circle. I was learning this in class, but I was not up to performance level, so I just held the groove. The rousing dance restored positive energy. Oba resumed teaching.

"Obatala asked Oludumare if he could come to Earth. Oludumare asked why. Obatala said, 'To make people worship You and praise You.' Oludumare gave permission. Orunmilla, who was the sacred witness to Oludumare's creation, asked, 'What will you need?' Obatala answered, 'A rooster with five legs,' and Orunmilla gave him one. Obatala came to Earth with the five-legged rooster. The rooster began digging and created five continents. That's how Obatala made the land.

"Next Obatala made the people out of clay. When the bodies wanted heads, Obatala asked Oludumare to put the breath of life into them. Obatala asked each person who he or she wanted to be and what he or she wanted to do on Earth. Some wanted to be animals. Each made a choice, then promptly forgot that choice. Orunmilla captured everyone's answer, so he can help people to remember their choice.

"Obatala got drunk on palm wine. He was tired but still wanted to keep making more people out of clay. He made some mistakes, and those are people who have birth defects. He said he would be their god and guide. That's why people who are physically deformed are often spiritually strong."

Oba grabbed his *djembe* and pounded out Rhumba, the rhythm that calls in all 400 orishas.[5] This rhythm provided the basis of Latin rumbas. The name was a contraction of a longer, tonal Yoruba phrase that was called out by the *babalawo* as a prelude to invoking the *orishas*. Unpronounceable by non-Yoruba speakers in the diaspora, the rhythm became commonly known by the simpler name, Rhumba. We jumped up and danced freely. High energy surged through us, but our movements were more restrained and proper than for Eshu. After all, Obatala is an old man. As usual, we danced for hours.

The more time I spent at Ifa Center, the more I became concerned that Miriam's management style was fatally flawed. When Oba would get hired for a gig, her favorite negotiating technique was to intentionally keep the terms of the contract as vague as possible. Then when payment was offered after the performance, she would act shocked at how little the amount was and accuse the client of being ungrateful and trying to cheat Oba. An argument ensued, which sometimes ended with a larger sum in her hand, but always ended with an alienated customer.

I wanted to help her make their business more successful, so I extolled the virtues of repeat business. Citing my background in film production, where fees and conditions are determined by union contracts, and deal memos are signed before any work begins, I tried to convince her of the value of clear, written agreements to ensure satisfied customers and positive word-of-mouth, but she would have none of it. The way she worked seemed to work for her. Maybe it was standard procedure in rough-and-tumble New York, but it did not play well in Zen California. She burned bridges. I talked to Oba about it, but he deferred to her as his manager. He felt business was not his forte, and he depended on her to get his jobs.

Miriam wanted to be seen as a spiritual queen to Oba's king, but she behaved like a scolding mother. In all fairness, Oba expected her to play bad cop to his good cop, but she relished the role far too much. Like Elegba, she loved to start arguments and stir up conflict. Miriam complained about how she wanted to create a spiritual community but people wouldn't do enough to help her. Yet when anyone in the community asked her for help, she demanded to be paid because she was running a business. When I said, "Miriam, I'm confused. Is it a business or a spiritual community? You can't have it both ways," she ignored me.

As I observed Oba and Miriam's marriage at close range, it wasn't pretty. At a meeting to discuss how to publicize Ifa Center, Miriam called Oba "stupid" and "lazy" in front of their inner circle. Oba made suggestions about how things should be done, and she brusquely vetoed them. She criticized him behind his back, complaining to me and other students that he didn't make enough money, although she was his business manager. She made a point of letting me know that their sex life was lacking. More than once, I overheard her telling other women that her marriage was sexless. The more she raged at Oba and his students for no apparent reason, the more I doubted her emotional stability.

Oba remained long-suffering, patient and kind in the face of her fury. When I encouraged him to stand up for himself, he emphasized that in his culture "keeping peace in the house" came first. This dynamic created a strong bond between Oba and his students because they felt sorry for him and despised Miriam's relentless persecutions, which fueled Miriam's anger because she perceived everyone as "on Oba's side" and "against" her. It was a difficult drama for me to watch, and I noticed other female students empathizing with Oba and wanting to rescue him.

On Oba's birthday, Bernadette, the Latina hottie, showed up with an elaborate birthday cake, set the candles ablaze and presented it to Oba singing a sexy "Happy Birthday" as though she was Marilyn Monroe to his JFK. After he blew out the candles, she told David that she was going to take him and his father to Disneyland. David was delighted. Miriam went berserk.

"You had no right to bake my husband a cake! You are not taking my son anywhere! David, you cannot go to Disneyland with this woman!"

Bernadette asked Miriam if she had baked a birthday cake. Miriam sputtered and insisted that she would do that later. I exchanged glances with sheepish Oba. Miriam turned to me and spewed, "How dare she?! How dare she?!"

I wished Oba "Happy Birthday" and excused myself. To me, it was absolutely obvious that Oba was sleeping with Bernadette.

Another woman, Devmata, spent most of every day at Ifa Center. Her son, Krishna, was the same age as David, and they played together, at least until Krishna would become violent and aggressive. Devmata was heavyset, mentally scattered and eager-to-please. She was a longtime Sikh devotee and still attended those services regularly. She was not East Indian. Like Miriam, she was Jewish and 40ish. Her birth name was Rebecca. She had two grown children by a Sikh leader, but Krishna's father was a Polynesian shaman who got her pregnant then disappeared. At every Saturday morning drum class, Devmata would come in late and interrupt the lesson to give Oba coffee. She wouldn't drum because she felt she wasn't any good at it. Oba encouraged her to play *djun djun*, but Devmata always declined. Miriam treated her like a slave and constantly badgered her to contribute more money. Devmata explained that she had no money and depended on food stamps, so Miriam confiscated the food stamps and went grocery shopping. My unspoken thought was: *Leave her alone. Do you know how poor you have to be to get food stamps?* However, one day Devmata produced a roll of bills, which she handed to Oba, and he counted with relish.

Devmata confided to me that she suspected Miriam suffered from mental illness, perhaps undiagnosed bi-polar disorder. She said she knew because she was a diagnosed, medicated bi-polar herself and also suffered from obsessive-compulsive disorder.

Oshun, Yemoja/Olokun, Shango

The Oshun river ceremony in Topanga Canyon was part of a summer solstice ritual that also honored the *orishas* Yemoja/Olokun and Shango. Oba instructed us to bring camping equipment and collect a container of seawater on our way to the location. Oba opened the day by chanting Ajaja as we danced our offerings of fruit up a path to a huge tent he'd built over an altar where flowers and candles surrounded a statue of Eshu in the guise of a monkey. A bottle of gin sat on the altar. Oba spilled some on the ground, "for the ancestors who have gone before us." Then he took a big swig and spit a spray over the altar. He took another swig, turned and spit the spray over all of us celebrants declaring, "Now you are one with Spirit." In ceremony, literal drinkable spirits can be a concretization of divine Spirit. At Oba's request, I smudged everyone with white sage smoke.

Oba led us in Eshu's chant and dance, then a masked dancer, called the Egungun, danced in holding a live chicken. The Egungun, a trance channel for ancestor spirits, rubbed the passive bird over each of us and asked it to take away our negativity. Later during the ceremony, the chicken laid an egg, and delighted children brought it up to the altar. The children were playful. Krishna was particularly rowdy and refused to listen to Miriam's scolding. Miriam grabbed his arm and delivered a cracking slap across his face. Devmata watched passively without comment.

Oba invited us to follow him, and the laughing band of

children, down a path to the Oshun altar beside the stream. We prayed with rose petals, washed, sang and danced until the goddess possessed us. After we recovered from being ridden by Oshun, we followed Oba and the children up the hill to an altar for Yemoja/Olokun.

Blue and white flowers and candles decorated this altar draped with blue and silver cloth. A galvanized tub with sand and shells on the bottom sat beside a statue of Yemoja/Olokun as a fierce mermaid with seaweed hair. Oba asked us to pour our containers of seawater into the tub to create a miniature ocean as he sang the chant invoking the double deity.[6]

"Yemoja/Olokun is the *orisha* of the ocean who expresses the energies of motherhood, prosperity and abundance," Oba explained. "Yemoja is the feminine aspect who appears as the mermaid. She is the sparkle of sun or moonlight on the water. The frothy white foam is the train of her dress. Olokun is the masculine aspect associated with cold depths and raging storms. He's a dark merman with tangled seaweed hair. Sharp fish hooks, torn nets and sunken ships surround him. Her colors are aqua blue, white and silver. His color is navy blue. They love blue and white flowers, silver coins, wine and honey. Yemoja's favorite offering is watermelon, for the sweetness of the water."

He taught us the dance to her song, Iyoya. We held a white handkerchief in each hand and placed our hands on our hips. With our weight on our right foot, we extended our left foot, tapped it to the beat, then jumped, landing with our weight on our left foot and rocked our pelvis like a boat bobbing in the surf. We tapped the right foot and repeated the movements. During the chorus, we stepped from side-to-side flipping the white handkerchiefs in the air. The handkerchiefs symbolize doves of peace being released. It's a dance for prosperity, since prosperity can only truly exist in times of peace. Iyoya, in the Bendel language from mid-western Nigeria, the tongue of a people who live by the ocean and are flooded at night by high tide, translates as "something good is coming, I can feel it." We bobbed and rocked into trance. I became the sea's cycling tides. Yemoja rode me.

As night fell, the men lit a fire at the altar for Shango. Oba disappeared and reappeared wearing a bright red hat with red and white beads over his white robes. Shango's colors are red and white. Oba chanted the invocation, "Shan-goooo!"[7] elongating the final vowel into a howl several times, then the drums broke into a swinging rhythm. Our hips swayed to Oba's chanting over the syncopated beat.

"Shango is the *orisha* of thunder, lightning and fire. He expresses the energies of anger, judgment, masculine leadership and manifestation," Oba said, illuminated only by flames. "He was a king, and when he opened his mouth, he spit fire. He is the cleansing fire of healing that burns off all the irregularities of life. He's also a judge, so his symbol is the gavel. He's a warrior, and the double-headed ax is his weapon. Women are attracted to his sexual heat. Offer him hot drinks, tobacco, chili peppers, red wine, whisky, alligator pepper and different kinds of kola nuts."

Oba translated the chant he sang next, "The fire of healing starts as a spark. We fan the flames until we are alive and well!" The beat started slowly. Oba sang, *"Weh reh weh reh nee nah jo."*[8] In a circle, we stepped from side to side, raising and lowering our arms. The beat picked up like a spark growing into fire. The tempo gradually moved faster, then a little faster, like flames leaping higher. The music stopped. Oba chanted, *"Ara mi lay. Ara mi lay!"* Suddenly, the drums burst into a frantic beat. Oba's chant jumped an octave higher and double-timed the tempo. We dancers stepped up our pace, scooting around the circle at full speed, pumping our arms wildly. I was alive and well! Shango's fire raged within me. I was possessed with righteous anger and healing heat. I felt like I was spitting flames.

When the ceremony ended, we went back to the Yemoja altar to wash ourselves and collect some seawater to take home. Then we ate a potluck feast and danced, laughed and sang until two in the morning. I crawled into my little tent exhausted. As I fell asleep, I felt at one with numinous Nature. At dawn, I awoke tingling with energy and in awe of the beauty of the ceremony. I felt deep appreciation for Oba's power to create community and his mastery of shamanism as public theater. Oba was the intoxicating leading man of a heady, exotic show.

Divination and Ebo

One afternoon when I had a moment alone with Oba, I asked, "What's Miriam's head?"

"Yemoja and Oya."

I recognized the ocean's mothering energy and the tornado's blistering fury in her.

"What's my head?"

"Oshun."

I was skeptical. I was no great beauty and certainly never thought of myself as a flowing love goddess. I'd expected him to characterize me as Oya, the furious truth-teller.

"I bet you say that to all the girls."

"No. You are Oshun," he said matter-of-factly.

Oba revealed that his head was Shango, which explained his masculine confidence and regal bearing. His dress, coloring and presence made him look like the darkest of the three wise men in Christian nativity scenes. Strangers on the street sometimes stopped him and asked to shake hands with "the king." But because Oba was a diviner, he was also ruled by Orunmilla. Oba explained that Orunmilla is not an *orisha*. In fact, he's not a being.

"He's energy that knows each of us: what each individual stands for and against. He's the original diviner who has witnessed everything we've agreed to."

Orunmilla is invoked at the beginning of every divination. The diviner needs his help. According to Oba, divining is critical to Ifa healing work. It doesn't foretell the future as much as it offers advice for balancing the archetypal energies.

"Divining does take the temperature of the future by revealing whether it's a good time for a certain action or what the chances are for a venture to be successful," said Oba.

He recommended divinations before weddings and other important life decisions. The result of a divination leaves the subject with homework in the form of rituals, ceremonies and/or offerings needed to bring the balance necessary for health, prosperity and harmonious relationships. The divination determines the subject's head *orisha* and suggests what actions must be taken to coax the future in the desired direction.

Offerings are called *"ebo."* They may be simple offerings, like tobacco, honey, flowers, candles, or, for the most difficult problems or important initiations, animal sacrifices such as chickens, doves or goats. I found this horrifying and asked Oba, "Why does Spirit want an animal to die? There must be a way to heal without taking another life."

"The animals have agreed to be our messengers to Spirit. Before we take their lives, we pray over them and ask them to take a message to Oludumare, like 'Please heal this person's disease' or 'Please make this marriage happy and successful.' We celebrate them during the ceremony. If we're celebrating an initiation or joyous occasion, we eat their meat to nourish the community. If the animal has been asked to take on an illness or misfortune, we do not eat them. Their lives are not wasted. They do us a great service, and we are deeply grateful."

I decided to keep an open mind. After all, I eat chickens that have not been prayed over or asked to carry a request to Spirit. I never saw Oba sacrifice an animal during ceremony. The killing and butchering took place in seclusion before the ritual. Oba marveled that Christians find animal sacrifice so objectionable.

"They hang a crucifix on their wall. Don't they realize that Jesus was a human sacrifice?"

Oba's divinations were elaborate, and his clients raved about their power. He asked the clients to bring in photos of their ancestors: parents, grandparents, aunts and uncles. Oba would build an altar that displayed these photos beside candles, flowers, smoking frankincense, water and other artifacts. After much chanting and praying, Oba "threw the shells" by shaking cowry shells in his cupped hands and dropping them into sand that filled the center of a circular divining tray. He divided the sand into four quadrants inside the carved rim. Where the shells fell in the quadrants, and whether they fell with rounded or cleft side up, indicated a numeric code that coordinated with passages in a book of Ifa scripture called the Odu, similar to how the pattern of cast coins coordinates with the verses of the I Ching.

The circular tray divided into four quadrants reminded me of the Native American medicine wheel. In both, the teaching and healing seeks the restoration of balance within the client. Ifa's similarity to Native American spirituality—and to the I Ching—provoked me to speculate that, at some point in prehistory, there may have been one proto-religion that migrated across the globe with humans.

After I'd attended Oba's classes and ceremonies for a year, he told me, "I want to see you." I was delighted that he wanted a more personal friendship, so I invited Oba and Miriam to dinner at my home. They accepted. I kept it casual, cooking pasta with broccoli and a vegetable pizza. They arrived an hour and a half late, carrying a sleeping David into my house and laying him on my sofa. I poured wine. As I served the food, Oba tactfully let me know that he couldn't digest cheese and hated vegetables. He didn't eat anything I'd prepared except bread and wine. It was late, and they were tired. Oba seemed oddly quiet. At the time, I attributed the awkward evening to the exhaustion of busy parents. Later, hidden subtext would be revealed.

I Wo San/Oya

Oba's *orisha* ceremonies incorporated I Wo San, one of the primary Ifa rituals. According to Oba, in Africa, Yoruba people celebrate I Wo San several times a year: at solstices and equinoxes, weddings and funerals, graduations and infant naming ceremonies as well as during *orisha* ceremonies. Whenever a community gathers for an important occasion, the I Wo San invokes the energies of the appropriate *orishas*, clarifies positive intention and honors the complexity of life. At the heart of I Wo San are offerings. Various tastes of life fill tiny white bowls that are passed around to all the celebrants as the *babalawo* explains their significance. These bowls serve as the focal point of the altar.

For Oya's ceremony, rich maroon fabric draped the walls of Ifa Center. We came bearing offerings of shiny purple eggplants, red wine and brandy. Oba appeared in a voluminous garment of maroon lace. A dog-ear hat shot with silver thread topped his head.

"Oya is the *orisha* of the wind, the whirlwind, the tornado. She stands for truth, feminine leadership and feminine fury. Because she is our breath, she lives in the graveyard and helps people cross over at the time of death. She rules the changes in our lives. Her sister is Oshun."

Oba added that her color is maroon but she also likes dark brown and deep purple, thus eggplant is her favorite offering. We danced in a circle as he chanted her song, Oya Ma Pa Mee[9], which translates, "When the wind blows and something is going to tear, let it tear. If it's going to break, let it break. When the wind is blowing, it has no respect for anybody."

He proceeded to the I Wo San. I passed the offerings to all the celebrants as Oba explained each one:

"Taste salt and honor the ocean, the mother who gave birth to us all. Taste your tears and your sweat." Each celebrant took a pinch and put it on their tongue.

"Taste bitter kola and honor the bitterness of life. As you chew on bitterness, remember to watch what you say because bitter kola makes spoken words manifest." Each celebrant took a piece of the medicinal, highly-caffeinated nut and chewed it. It tasted acrid and nasty.

"Taste honey and honor the sweetness that Nature provides us." Each celebrant dipped a finger in honey and licked it.

"Taste alligator pepper, and appreciate the spice of life." He instructed men to take seven peppercorns and women to take five, and all wait until everyone had the pepper in hand. Then he told everyone to put the potent red pepper in their mouths at the same time, chew three times, and inhale in unison. We felt the heat together.

"Taste palm oil and honor what blends things together and makes them go smoothly." Celebrants dipped a finger in the greasy orange goo and touched it to their lips.

"Taste sugar in the shape of a house and honor the sweetness man creates." Each celebrant took a sugar cube and ate it.

"Taste water and honor how it purifies, cools and creates peace of mind. Accept the blessing of Oshun, the *orisha* of love."

He sprinkled each celebrant's face with water. Then he passed his hand over the bowl, and a flame ignited in the middle of the water.

"Behold the fire in the water! Know that the impossible is possible. See how opposites can come together as one."

(Later, after I became Oba's confidant, he showed me how he performed this magician's trick. He concealed a small cube of naphtha in his hand, then deftly lit it and floated it in the bowl of water.)

Then Oba took a special divining kola nut, sprinkled it with water, broke it into pieces, threw the segments on the altar and read a message for the celebrants. It was a positive message. Our intentions were good. The crowd cheered! The drums rolled!

Oba led the drummers in Oya's rhythm. Then he demonstrated her dance, spinning one way, then changing direction. Following his lead, we spun and swirled like cyclones until the trance took us. I felt the power of the tornado enter me. I became blind destruction. Oya rode me until I was furious, feminine truth.

In all these *orisha* ceremonies, Oba shone like a superstar. He was at home when he was center stage. He deftly guided group energy, raising it to a fever pitch, then calming it down with ease. Everyone participated. He cajoled would-be observers into joining the dance by playfully threatening to write them a ticket for staying on the sidelines. Everyone bathed in his love. All the men wanted to be his favorite friend, and of course, all the women were in love with him. He reveled in the feminine attention, much to Miriam's frustration.

As much as I, too, was dazzled by Oba's charisma, I was equally attracted to the practice of Ifa. The drumming connected me to my own heartbeat. The dance connected me to my body and my libido. The trance connected me to the supernatural. The ceremonies connected me to the energies of Nature. The entire spiritual technology connected me to life and placed me firmly on the earth.

After a ceremony at Ifa Center, Oba walked me to my car and asked, "Can I come and see you?" Obviously, he didn't want his wife to hear. Suddenly I got it! He was hitting on me. He didn't want to be invited to my dinner parties. He wanted to be my lover. I knew I should be outraged by a married man's advances, but truth be told, I really wanted to go to bed with him.

"Yes. Just call me before you come."

In fact, I had already struggled with, agonized over—and resolved in my own mind—the moral and ethical dilemma around having an affair with a married man.

When I was younger, I was horrified when married men hit on me. The year before, one of Archer's students, whom I knew was married, propositioned me. I went to my teacher indignant and told him that I was shocked that someone who was supposed to be spiritual would attempt to cheat on his wife. Of course, I was expecting to be praised for resisting temptation, so I was caught off-guard by my teacher's response.

"Are you attracted to him?"

The man, Arjuna, was a handsome, intelligent Asian healer.

"Yes."

"If the idea of being his lover interests you, I think you should explore it."

I protested that adultery was wrong and that I would be betraying his wife (although I didn't know her).

Archer responded, "Monogamy is a cultural convention. Polygamy is much more common throughout the world. My own mother came from a matrilineal culture where women had more than one husband. Judging other family structures as wrong is simply narrow-minded. Even in our culture, people get unmarried and find new partners all the time."

Although I was taken aback, I was willing to reconsider my position. Eventually, I succumbed to Arjuna's advances. We had been involved in a tumultuous long-distance relationship for over a year. He lived in Arizona but came to see me when he visited his parents in Southern California. I saw him when I went to Arizona to study with Archer. Intense phone conversations kept us close despite long separations, but when we were together, conflicts sparked. He claimed he simply intended to explore a sexual relationship outside his long-term marriage, but I recognized that our relationship allowed both of us to act out our shadow.

Another reason I was open to sleeping with married men was that monogamy didn't work particularly well for me. Although I was faithful throughout my 18-year marriage, my husband was not, and I felt the strain of temptation. My mind, heart and experience told me that monogamy becomes unrealistic in long-term relationships. Throughout my adult life, I'd witnessed the failures of many friends' marriages due to the husbands' infidelity.

I wondered if men's infidelity expresses their unique wisdom. Maybe they know that monogamy is a sham that just makes everyone unhappy. Is men's infidelity simply a mirror to show women that we too would like to have multiple partners, or at least serial partners? Is men's lack of monogamy such a hot button for women because men have betrayed our trust, or because we don't want to be monogamous either? Or both? Are men unfaithful? Or are they faithful to a deeper truth that our culture wants to keep hidden? Could men and women find the courage to live that deeper truth openly?

I speculated on the origin of monogamy and decided that, in pre-agricultural times, the nuclear family would not have been a successful strategy for survival. Too many women died in childbirth and too many men were killed in accidents and war for a one man/one woman-caring-for-their-children model to evolve. A clan of many women, who could nurse orphaned children and live on their own subsistence farming and wild-gathering, would make much more sense. In such a clan, only one really virile man would be necessary to father children (or maybe a couple of them to diversify the gene pool). All the other men would become dispensable and could be assigned dangerous tasks like hunting and fighting. It would take a village of lots of women and a few potent men to keep life going. Hence, polygamy would evolve.

Perhaps unconscious knowledge that most men are dispensable creates the human male's primal wound of powerlessness which generates his need to control and dominate the family, the opposite sex, his children and every social structure. And perhaps the buried memory of the old communal way of life explains why women tend to be cooperative. Cooperation among women insured survival. In a strong sisterhood, a child's paternity would be irrelevant information.

In the *New York Times* bestseller *Sex at Dawn: The Prehistoric*

Origins of Modern Sexuality, author/researchers Christopher Ryan and Cacilda Jetha describe prehistoric hunter-gatherers living in egalitarian matriarchal clans of less than 150 people. All members of the group shared food, childcare and sex partners. Elder females used sex to create bonding and calm aggressive young males. The authors propose that ancestral memory of this ancient lifestyle creates our current struggles around living in monogamous nuclear families.

Even today, the Mosuo culture of China practices "walking marriage." The Mosuo live in extended matrilineal families. Women of childbearing age have rooms with a door opening to the street. These women can invite men to spend the night with them. Those men walk from their house to the woman's room at night and walk back to their home in the early morning. A Mosuo woman can change partners as often as she likes without social stigma, but in fact, few women have more than one partner at a time. The man will never go to live in the woman's family or vice versa. Couples never share property. A man participates in the support and care of children born to his mother's family. His children stay with their mother's family. A child may never know who his or her father is but will be raised with many caring uncles and aunts. This system creates an extremely stable family structure with no divorce or child custody issues. If a parent dies, the large extended family cares for the child.

Ryan and Jetha conclude that monogamy must have evolved along with agriculture and the concept of property ownership. When alpha males began to acquire land and wealth, they would have wanted to know that they were passing it on to their own children. Women exchanged their shared power for borrowed power bestowed by a man who promised to take care of one woman and their children in exchange for monogamy. It was a devil's bargain. Men could easily conspire to evade it. Women were (and still are) stoned to death for adultery.

Oba came from a polygamous culture. Miriam tried to deny

this every time the topic came up. She insisted that Oba's siblings assured her that their family was monogamous, although some Yorubas are polygamous. Behind her back, Oba explained that when he was a child his mother moved to northern Nigeria alone, because she didn't want any more children, and his father continued to have children with younger women. Oba claimed that he had no idea how many stepbrothers and stepsisters he had and that his father was still "on active duty" well into his 90s. Oba pointed to the amorous adventures recounted in the *orisha* stories as evidence that polygamy was part of Yoruba culture. I noted the 1978 marriage of Afrobeat musician and activist Fela Kuti to 27 wives during one ceremony as a demonstration of this phenomenon.

From my point of view, monogamy didn't work. Polygamy, documented in the Bible, is still widely practiced throughout Africa and Asia, and it persists among Mormon fundamentalists in contemporary America. In fact, far more cultures worldwide embrace polygamy than monogamy. Of the 1,231 cultures described in the *Ethnographic Atlas Codebook as of 2011*, 84.6 percent are classified as polygynous (one husband, multiple wives), 15.1 percent as monogamous (one husband, one wife), and 0.3 percent as polyandrous (one wife, multiple husbands). If it was just a cultural difference, I was willing to give it a try.

I also thought having a part-time husband might work well for me. I knew I needed solitude, and marriage stole it from me. Being unable to escape my husband's neediness left me drained. I needed time alone to take care of myself, and I also needed companionship, intimacy and sex. Rather than 24/7 marriage, I thought I'd prefer a loose alliance where both parties were free to create their own happiness, coming and going as needed. Why should exclusivity be a given? Shouldn't it be negotiable depending on the situation and people involved?

Finally, I believed that Oba was in a miserable marriage. I didn't want to hurt Miriam, but I could see that she had already ruined her relationship with her husband. I had no intention of wrecking Miriam's home, but if she believed her relationship was monogamous, and Oba wanted to be polygamous, their relationship was doomed no matter what I did. At that time, I saw Oba as a glorious songbird in the clutches of a vicious harridan.

Two days after our encounter in the parking lot, Oba left a message on my voicemail in Yoruba. The only words I recognized were my name and "Oshun." I assumed it was a prayer asking Oshun to bring me to him. Later, I would wonder if that invocation was a spell putting me in Oshun's power.

When Oba called the next day, he told me he'd divined for himself and seen that we were supposed to be together. He told me Oshun ruled my head. I was the Oshun to his Shango. He told me he'd found out his mother had died a few days earlier. He felt the fact that we were getting together just after her death meant I was her choice for him.

At that moment, his words penetrated deep into my heart. Some disowned part of me was waiting for a powerful spiritual partner. Oba seemed to be that man. The high communion of our souls promised to be the culmination of my quest to bring the races together. Like Oshun and Shango, our divine love transcended the complications of conventional morality. He was anointing me as his special one.

He aroused me with a tantalizing story:

As Oshun bathes in a river, she notices Shango watching her from a hiding place in the jungle. Although she knows Shango is married to Oya, she lures Shango to riverbank, and asks him, "Can you please help me? I put this honey on my skin to make it soft and smooth, but I can't reach my back. Could you rub it on me?" Shango says, "Of course." Shango rubs honey on her back, her shoulders, her neck, her thighs, her breasts. He kisses her. She kisses him. They make hot and tender love on the cool, moist riverbank.

Later, I would recognize that this divine soap opera of Oshun,

Shango, Oya and Ogun is the core myth of Yoruba spirituality. At the time, I didn't realize that Oba was living his faith by embodying the mythological story. He cast himself as alpha male Shango and was offering me the role of adulterous temptress Oshun.

Oba said he'd come over in an hour. I jumped in the shower and put on a sexy white sundress. While I was waiting for him to arrive, the phone rang. I answered.

"Hi, Marsha, It's Miriam."

I scrambled for what to say, not knowing if she would confront me... or what?

She just wanted to talk, and I was expecting her husband to walk in my door any minute! She told me about her problems with her mother. She told me about Oba's family in Nigeria, and how his mother just died and hadn't been buried yet because the family wanted him there to officiate at her funeral, but he couldn't afford to go. She told me about how his sister adopted his three daughters by different women. My life was getting curiouser and curiouser.

Oba knocked on the door, and I told Miriam that I had company and had to get off the phone. As I hung up the phone and opened the door, Eshu pushed me.

Oba entered, embracing me, kissing me, telling me he loved me. I said, "I don't want Miriam to get hurt."

"Since David was born seven years ago, the feeling between me and Miriam has gone. We were good together in New York, but since we've been in L.A., she worries about everything and doesn't want to be touched, so we go months without having sex."

Miriam had told me as much herself. Oba revealed that he'd been attracted to me since the healing vigil and had been afraid to approach.

"You have what makes me feel good again, what keeps me going."

I was surprised to hear him confess to having a hard time. To me he was always glowing with joy. He said he wanted to take me to Nigeria with him some day to show me Lagos.

"Oba, you should know that marriage just didn't work for me. I think I'm happier when I have more than one man. I'm seeing someone once in a while now. He's married too."

I asked him if Bernadette was his girlfriend. He denied it. I knew he was lying, but I let it go in the heat of the moment, foolishly assuming he would tell me the truth once he knew he could trust me.

He prayed in Yoruba and had me repeat it in English.

"I wish you prosperity. I wish you children. I wish you health."

I repeated it, but said, "Oba, I don't want children."

"You have children everywhere, and children don't come when you want them. They come when they want to."

"Do you hear me? I don't want children. You leave children behind you everywhere you go. You must be very careful with me."

"I will be careful."

Then, two years after I first met him, a year after I started taking his classes, we made love. He was passionate, urgent, desperate to get inside me. I melted against his luscious chocolate skin and got lost in the soft fuzz under his locks. I insisted that he use a condom. He resisted at first but finally capitulated. Oshun came alive in our bodies. His fire burned so hot that he finished before me. I showed him how to help me climax. He got the idea, but it might have been new to him. After our crescendos, we laid in each other's arms.

To me, these moments of comfort and communion in the afterglow were as transcendent as the moment of orgasm, but Oba didn't stay long. He was off to sing at a recording session. He took a shower. I offered him fruit. We kissed, touched and danced sensuously before he left.

Oba was right. I am Oshun. I love sex. That doesn't mean that I want to sleep with every man I see. It means that when I find chemistry, intimacy and real connection with a partner who cares about me, has lovemaking skills and makes my pleasure as important as his own, I love sex. I'd been with less than a dozen men in my life. I'd had a few one-night stands, and that's how I knew casual sex didn't work for me.

I always enjoyed sex with my husband. Even when every other aspect of the relationship was dysfunctional, we were good in bed. Sex since my divorce had been scarce and disappointing. The few partners I'd had were short on skill and enthusiasm. A lover with Oba's sexual energy and passion was rare and valuable. I was swept away in the river of love and desire.

At the next ceremony, I got no special attention, and Oba behaved like a good husband toward Miriam. He was so convincing, I began to wonder if he was backing away from me. When I got home and crawled into bed at 2 a.m., the phone rang. It was Oba saying he loved me and wanted to say goodnight before I went to sleep. He called again the next day saying he wanted to see me again and asked about my schedule for the coming week. He called the next morning and left a message saying, "Good morning," that he loved me and would call later.

I was in love with Oba, but I was also in love with the throbbing drums, the sensuous dance, the beauty of ceremony, the energies of the *orishas*, the exotic ancient wisdom. I couldn't separate these loves.

Each time we made love, it got better. His sweat smelled of frankincense and glazed his ebony body like a sacred resin. His hands were calloused, hard as wood, from centuries of drumming. In his strong black hands, my breasts became huge precious pearls. As he entered me, I received the blessing of Oshun. My sexual self came alive again.

Oba called at least once a day. I was afraid that Miriam would see the phone bills and figure it out, but then Miriam called me almost once a day herself. The closer I got to Oba, the closer I got to Miriam. Oba said, "That's part of the miracle." I asked him what we would do if we were in Nigeria. He said he'd just take me as a second wife, and we'd all get along. I thought that might work for me, but I knew it would never work for Miriam.

Oba was a midnight rambler. He would show up at my door between 10 and midnight. We'd talk, drink wine, massage each other, make love, take a shower together. Then he'd disappear into the night around two in the morning. He said he had to be home by three because that's when he did his prayers and divinations. When I voiced my need for him use a condom, he complied immediately, saying if that's what I needed, that's what he would do.

Sex defined the relationship, for both of us, and that was OK. We were both delighted to find a partner who matched our level of sexual energy. He didn't have Arjuna's technique, but he was wonderfully passionate and appreciative of me. While I worked on teaching him skills between the sheets, I enjoyed his raw passion. He was a quick study and mastered the art of simultaneous orgasm in a few sessions. I suspected that he had other women, but he'd been clear that he came from a polygamous tradition. Oba seemed to have many answers for my questions about life. At this point in the game, I was entertaining the possibility that polygamy might be one of those answers.

Ogun

"Oshun and Ogun are married, but they are complete opposites," Oba told us during the ceremony for Ogun, *orisha* of iron and war. "Ogun is a forceful macho man. Oshun is soft, loving and caring. Ogun hates that it takes Oshun two or three hours to dress. He is speedy like a car or train. Oshun is quiet like water. Ogun is noisy like a machine, strong and forceful. He punishes you for mistakes. Oshun is gentle and forgiving. They don't get along. At the same time, Oshun always has her eyes on

Shango, a powerful king who is not as mean and fierce as Ogun. Police and soldiers are children of Ogun. They carry out Shango's orders because he is a judge. Shango is married to Oya, sister of Oshun. Oya is the power behind Shango's throne. Shango determines the balance between opposite forces and tips the scale. Debate in the courtroom is the furious energy of Oya's whirlwind. Shango needs Oya to tell him where to throw his thunderbolts. Oshun lures him in."

Dark green fabric covered the walls. The color symbolizes the forest where Ogun goes to live alone and atone for killing innocent people in hot-tempered rage. Oba wore green glass beads over his white robes and a green velvet hat. A fanciful-yet-fearsome assemblage of iron objects served as Ogun's altar. Rusted gears, knives, nails, caldrons, forks, bicycle parts, kitchen pots, railroad spikes and vicious machetes balanced precariously and poked threateningly in the dim candlelight. We gave Ogun offerings of hot chili peppers, cigars, rum and red palm oil.

"Ogun embodies the energies of aggression and protection. He rules the physical energy that moves our bodies. With his machete, he clears our path of obstacles. He's a warrior who lives in the forest. He's represented as a man on a horse with a gun or a machete and a loyal dog," Oba explained, then broke into the song, Ogun La Kayay[10], which translates as, "The grass on the riverbank is always green," a metaphor for Ogun's eternal nature. He started with an *a capella* chant, then drums joined in with a chugging rhythm evoking a speeding train. Dancers moved their arms like spinning locomotive wheels or mimed swinging a machete to clear their path of obstacles.

"Ogun often travels with his brother, Ochosi, a lesser *orisha* of the hunt. He's an archer who lives in the forest," Oba continues. "Because he doesn't have to aim to hit the target, Ochosi expresses intuition and shamanic power. His symbol is the bow and arrow. If you are a hunter or fisherman, you honor Ogun but also offer major songs and *ebo* to Ochosi. Sometimes Ogun and

Ochosi merge into one *orisha*."

Because we would return home in our cars, which are made of iron, Oba always chanted Ogun's song, Ile Re Ogun[11], as the finale of every ceremony. The song asks Ogun to protect all the celebrants. Ogun replies, "I will do the damage, and I will repair it." Oba called Ogun's name in a familiar way, "Ogun-o," then extended the final vowel into a sustained note, "Ogun-ooooooo!" The drums started a slow beat as Oba sang the chorus.

"Ogun Karanga. Karanga-ay. I Yi Yi Yi Karanaga, Karanga-ay!"

Dancers moved freely. Hips undulated. Outstretched thumbs mimed hitchhiking. Oba seduced everyone into joining his joyous cry of "Ogun-oooooooo!" The tempo moved faster. We laughed with Oba. Dancers went wild! We were hunters! We were warriors! We connected with other dancers, then separated and found new partners, checking out promising couplings and potential rides home. Rhythm and movement escalated into frenzy. A final series of staccato drum slaps signaled sudden silence. After a few moments of stillness, drummers and dancers slipped away into the night.

Chapter 2

Playing at Polygamy

October 1994

Arjuna called before eight in the morning and showed up at noon. We went to bed immediately. He asked, "Can we do this without having a fight first?"

"We can have a fight if that's what gets you hot."

He said it wasn't, and we spent a sweet hour and a half making love. Damn, he was good, technically accomplished and profoundly sensuous. As we were dressing, I said, "Arjuna, you are an incomparable lover, and I really enjoy being in bed with you."

"You're not so bad yourself."

He complimented me on being inexhaustible. I told him I had another lover and described my relationship with Oba. Arjuna had no objection. In fact, he said he thought it was healthy and gave me unsolicited advice.

"Your attitude has a lot of control over what happens. You know what to do. Just don't go into your head trying to analyze it."

"Sometimes I get scared because Oba's crazy love for me makes me worry that he's a loose cannon."

"That's how I felt about you at first. You've been on both sides now. You can understand him."

Arjuna was eager to get back to Arizona because he and his wife were moving to a new house.

"I better go before you start sizzling again."

It didn't sit right with me that the wives of my lovers were being deceived. If it was my decision alone, I'd have chosen to let everyone involved know what was going on, but I put my ear in the soup and agreed to be a party to their deception. My excuse was that since I wasn't married, I wasn't breaking any vows, and I wasn't responsible for making other people keep the vows they chose to make.

How did having two lovers feel to me? Deceptions aside, it felt easy and natural.

November 1994

Oba told me that he'd come to see me at 10 p.m. but didn't show up until 1:30 a.m. He needed to be home by three to do his daily prayers, so we made love in a rush. He finished before me, got up, went in the bathroom and turned on the shower. I called him back to bed and told him I wasn't finished. He apologized and returned to bed. I tried, but I knew he wanted to leave, so I was distracted.

"Go ahead, it's all right."

"Are you mad at Oba?"

"When you leave without taking care of me, I feel like you don't care about me."

"No way! I care very much about you. There just isn't enough time. Forgive me this time. Next time I'll allow plenty of time."

"I forgive you."

"Sometime I'll get mad at you too."

It wasn't a threat, simply an acknowledgment that these things happen in relationships. Before he left, I asked him why he always took a shower after sex. He said it was a religious ritual to honor Oshun.

The next time Oba called I explained that, although I wasn't mad at him, I felt disrespected when he didn't allow enough time to make love to me properly. I asked him not to come see me expecting sex unless he could spend two hours. He agreed to my two-hour rule.

Every time I had a private conversation with Miriam, she made a point of telling me that she "just doesn't feel sexual" so she and Oba never made love. I would always steer the conversation away from such treacherous ground, but I often overheard her telling other women the same story.

The next time she brought it up, I said, "Miriam, that's really dangerous. Men need sex. If they are not getting it at home, they will get it somewhere else. When you tell all the women at Ifa Center that you are not having sex with Oba, you are practically inviting them to sleep with your husband. In fact, every time you tell me, I think, 'My God, there's a gorgeous man going to waste.'"

She looked terrified and changed the subject. From her reaction, I guessed that what I'd said may have had more truth than I knew. Perhaps she pimped out her husband to bring additional income into the house. The most likely suspects, Bernadette and Devmata, did contribute generously. As long as the sex stayed secret, maybe she didn't mind. I wondered what would happen if I revealed my secret affair with her husband. At that moment, I didn't have the courage to find out.

The next weekend, she told me that she and Oba had sex during the week. She said that Oba was the best sex partner she'd ever had, and she saw the irony in how she was unable to appreciate him. I deftly dropped the subject. Later, I mentioned it to Oba, and he denied it. He said they definitely hadn't had any sex at all in more than a month.

"We are not even sleeping together! I sleep on the living room floor because she complains about being crowded in bed."

I didn't know who to believe. Oba might have been feeling defensive, but Miriam's story seemed to have been spun for my benefit.

Before we made love, I assured Oba that it was OK with me if he had sex with his wife. I wanted him to be happy. Having a better relationship with her would make his life better. He said he understood and assured me that his relationship with her had improved since he'd been seeing me, because he was less tense and needy. He explained that he understood why she was the way she was and that's what allowed him to continue living with her.

"Do you understand why I am the way I am? What makes me angry? What I need?"

"I'm learning you, like I'm learning your body."

We made love slowly and sweetly. His skin, like dark silk, slid beneath my fingers, against my cheek, between my thighs. I tasted distant lands dripping with humidity, throbbing to the rhythm of drums. His dense dreadlocks spoke with the scent of strange spices. His touch took me into unknown territory. I explored the flow of Oshun in me, the fire of Shango in him.

Our sexual chemistry was undeniable, but I also felt a profound affection growing in me, and I saw it in him too. Oba said that he and I understood life in the same way. In that moment, I believed it. I wanted to be that special one who was most like him.

Sometimes when we made love, Oba tried to enter me without a condom. I would stop him and ask him to put one on.

"I'm not coming yet."

"I know, but I worry. You're too powerful a man, and you have too many children. It's for AIDS too. You don't know who else I'm sleeping with."

He would say he understood, but he would lose his erection. I'd be upset for a week. He was forcing me to be the parent, the responsible one, the condom police. I resented it. It set a pattern that could create the same kind of relationship that he had with Miriam. I also resented that he refused to give me oral sex, although he enjoyed it thoroughly when I offered it to him. When I requested it, he told me it was taboo for him because as a priest he "prays with his mouth." I was skeptical. He assured me that if we were in Africa, it would be different because he would have access to particular cleansing herbs. I suspected he was taking advantage of the culture gap, since I had no way to verify his story.

And yet, I loved that he left tender phone messages for me when I was working long hours. He thought about me and prayed for me even when I didn't have time for him. I'd never been loved like that in my life.

1995

"You and I are stuck to each other now," Oba said in the afterglow of delicious sex. It felt true in my bones. As he was leaving my bed, he said, "I will love you forever!"

"Forever? Coming from a man who has four children by four different women? Let's just say we love each other now."

I asked Oba if he would like to have another child.

"Yes, I like having children because they are more of you."

"Is that why you resist using condoms? Because you really want to get me pregnant?"

He didn't deny it.

"You need a younger woman. Maybe when you get rich, you can get a young wife who can give you lots of children. Would you like that?"

"Yes."

"Miriam probably doesn't want to have sex with you now because she's afraid of getting pregnant. What kind of birth control do you use?"

"Just condoms, but I don't like using them because I don't get the feeling I want."

"Then you're not getting it with me either."

He shrugged.

"You men always complain about not getting enough sex, but if you'd take responsibility for birth control, you could have a lot more sex."

"I see you understand us."

"And you understand me."

March 1995

I brought up the subject of getting HIV tests so we could use different kinds of contraception. Oba said he had one when he got married six years ago, and it was negative.

"Have you been with anyone other than Miriam since?"

"No."

I wanted to believe him, but I didn't.

"I need us to be tested just to be sure."

"It would be nice not have to use condoms, but it's OK to continue with them too."

"I know I've made it clear to you that if you have sex with someone else, I want you to tell me, but you've never told me whether or not you want me to tell you."

His pause revealed that I'd touched a painful subject.

"You don't have to tell me. I know."

The next day, he called.

"I realize I didn't answer your question. Of course, I know that a woman as beautiful as you would have other men in love with her."

Good answer!

"I only asked because I don't want to lie to you, but I don't want to hurt you either. So here's the deal. I have a lover who lives in Arizona. I see him once in a while. It doesn't mean I don't love you. I do love you, and I love him too in a different way. It's probably something like the way you love me and you love Miriam too but differently. He's married too, and he doesn't want to leave his wife, and I don't want him to. I wouldn't want to live with him, because I think we'd fight too much. That's all I'm going to say about it unless you ask me. And I want you to be honest with me about your other lovers in the same way I've been honest with you."

Oba laughed and said "OK."

April 1995

Oba landed a part in a movie and flew off to a location in Texas on short notice, playing an African witch doctor as a foil for a popular comedian. As if on cue, Arjuna appeared as Oba exited. We made love for hours. Oba called me daily from Texas assuring me that he missed me and couldn't wait to see me again. Arjuna spent the night and drove away towards Arizona in the morning. That evening, Oba called and said he was coming home the next day.

"I've never felt the way I feel about you. I couldn't sleep last night just thinking about seeing you again."

"Is that true? You didn't feel this with all the other women you've been in love with, all your other wives?"

"No, I've never been in love like this."

I almost believed him. I wanted to believe that I was the special one whom he loved like he'd never loved anyone before. When he came over the next day, we talked and had sweet, sweaty sex.

That night he was scheduled to perform at a ceremony for the third anniversary of the healing vigil. I was already at the location when he arrived with an entourage, including a young woman, Yvonne, one of his drumming students, a petite, slender brunette in her late 20s. As he entered with her on his arm, she looked up at him worshipfully. My intuition told me she was his lover too.

I decided to leave after his performance. As I was walking down a deserted hall toward the exit, he stepped out of a darkened room and greeted me. We embraced, and he walked with me. Yvonne appeared out of the same room, looking uneasy. I felt a twinge in my gut and realized they'd been making out in that room. Later I tried to deny it and told myself I was just jealous. Then I thought: *No... that's your gut. Pay attention to it.*

Did he go directly from my bed to hers, just as I went from Arjuna to him?

After a drum class, Miriam told me she'd realized that, in the past, she had a pattern of attracting deceitful men who abandoned her. She saw that she'd been projecting that pattern on the guys at Ifa Center. I said, "It's good that you recognize that," but I was thinking: *Oh my God, if she only knew how she's still in the pattern!* She said she was glad she found Oba who is not like that. *Oh my God, yes he is.* Then she told me that the thing she felt worst about was that she'd lost her sense of herself as a sexual, sensual person. She just hadn't felt it lately and wanted to get it back. *Oh my God, she's confiding in me, and I'm fucking her husband!* I said, "You must work on that. You can't expect a man to go indefinitely without sex. It's inviting disaster."

I left with my head spinning. Oba walked me to my car, and I told him about the conversation:

"I feel like I've fallen through the looking glass—and I'm going straight to hell!"

"Sometimes I feel like that too."

"If she ever finds out, she'll be completely devastated."

"Things like that happen to people all the time, and they live through it."

I decided that we had to tell Miriam. Then I decided that was a bad idea because Miriam punished people when they told her the truth. Like one day when she found a crayon mark on a pillowcase, she accused David of doing the damage. He denied it. She screamed, "Don't lie to me!" and kept badgering him until he admitted that he'd been coloring on the bed. Then she attacked him with a fury: screaming, denigrating, spanking and finally punishing him by taking away his crayons. I thought: *No wonder he lies to you, look what happens when he tells the truth.* I decided that I was definitely the wrong confidant for Miriam. She needed a therapist.

I was not at Ifa Center when one of the women students took Miriam aside and told her that Oba had been having an affair with Bernadette for a year and a half. Outraged, Miriam insisted that Bernadette was lying. Then the woman, Linda, a sensible matron, confronted Oba, and he tried to convince her it wasn't true. I thought *Of course he's having an affair with Bernadette, just like he's having an affair with me, and Yvonne, and God knows who else.*

The only thing I'd asked of Oba was honesty, and he'd been lying to me all along. As I watched his House of Love come crashing down, I hoped getting caught in the web of his own lies would teach him a lesson. I felt the impulse to tell Miriam that I'd been sleeping with Oba, but if I did, she'd certainly call me a liar too. I knew I had to cut it off with him. I was part of the deception. I needed to stop lying.

At that time, I realized that Oba was out of integrity with his spirituality and his culture, but I had the arrogance to think I could rescue him. Surely, this glorious healer had just lost his way among the unfamiliar customs of a foreign land. I believed my love would guide him back to his original truth. I didn't see that Oba had a different definition of integrity. In his world, he found spiritual integrity by embodying and living the energies of the *orishas*, who lie and deceive in their core myths. He was in integrity with the divinities that possessed him. I did not understand this, even though I justified my actions by identifying with the adulterous goddess Oshun.

I knew that when I confronted Oba he would deny everything and convince me that all these women wronged him. I wanted evidence, confirmed by an outside source that I trusted, so I could be absolutely sure he lied to me. I called Asante, my sacred sister from many sweatlodges. I knew she'd keep my secret. She told me that she knew for sure of at least one other person who slept with Oba but called it off. Asante offered me advice.

"We women must force men to be honest and take responsibility, in a loving way, while continuing to stay in relationship with them."

When Oba showed up, I said, "Oba, there's a lot to talk about."

"I know. You're concerned about what Linda said. I could hear it in your voice."

"What would you have said if Linda told Miriam she knew you were having an affair with me?"

"That's supposed to be just between us."

"It is, but what if that was what she said?"

"Then I'd say, 'Yes, it's true.'"

"In my mind, for you to swear to Linda and Miriam that you are not having an affair, when you are having one with me, is lying. Linda is on the right track, she just has the name wrong."

I added that for me to look Miriam in the eye when she was telling me she was so glad she was married to Oba because she knew he would never deceive her, when I knew he was deceiving her by having an affair with me, meant I was lying too.

"Oba, I just can't do it. I need to take responsibility for my own actions. I know that I have been dishonest."

"I have too."

"I know I have been sexually greedy."

"I have too."

"I know I have been willing to hurt someone else to get what I want."

"I have too."

"I need to stop doing those things. I need to stop having sex with you for now, and because I'm not sure whether or not you've been with Bernadette, I won't have sex with anyone for three months and then get an HIV test."

"I will do that too."

Later he backpedaled saying I should just go and get the test.

"I'm confused. You said you'd do it, and now you're trying to get out of it."

He said it would cost money, and it didn't seem necessary. I explained it wasn't just about the test, but it was more about giving the other person the gift of being sure they were safe with you. He said he understood and would do it.

He was supportive of my decision to be celibate: no rage, no trying to manipulate me into sex, no physical force, no begging for a mercy fuck. He handled it with equanimity, reason and understanding, but he also didn't confess anything. He stuck to his story that I was the only woman he'd been to bed with since his marriage. I reiterated the importance of honesty with me.

"God and the *orishas* know if you are telling the truth."

"Yes, they do."

I talked about abuse of power by priests and the harm done when women came for healing and were used for sex. He said he understood and agreed but swore he didn't do that.

"But you have to look at my background."

"Yes. In your background, you have four children by four different women."

"Yes, but I come from a polygamous culture. When you go to take a second wife, you don't just walk up to someone on the street and ask them. You start a relationship 'in the shade.' When you're sure it works, and it's what you want, you go to your first wife's parents and tell them you want to take a second wife, and they tell her. That's what I'm doing with you."

That made some sense to me, but I wanted him to admit he was auditioning other relationships too. I'd been honest with him about my other relationship. I wanted him to man up and be honest with me. I wondered if he would stay interested when no sex was involved.

May 1995

During our hiatus, Oba still came to visit me. He was completely present and never tried to make it sexual. He didn't make me wrong or try to talk me out of what I needed to do. He didn't tell me I was hysterical or crazy. Even when we were separated, Oba stayed in the myth, feeling divine longing for me, his Oshun.

I kept attending Oba's classes. One Saturday, Bernadette showed up glowing, accompanied by a girlfriend. They stood around and watched the class like she was showing off Oba to her friend. Yvonne floated around like a smug little princess. Devmata brought Oba coffee "just the way he likes it." Miriam marched in and acted like the queen of it all. I watched everything and hated myself for falling for his bullshit just like all the rest of them. I'd let him lie to me just because I wanted to be loved. Oba was in control, the director of this drama. He'd cast himself as Shango and assigned the parts of the different goddesses to all these women. Just like me, each of these women bought the story that she was the special one.

The next time Oba called, he was all charm. I snapped.

"It made me sick to see you with all your women. I feel stupid that I'm one of them. Don't call me anymore unless you're going to start being honest with me."

"What do you want from me? Do you want me to tell you I'm having sex with women that I'm not having sex with? Will that make you happy?"

We fought. The next morning, I woke up feeling confused. Was I right? Or was I projecting my fear that I was unlovable on him? I wanted to be respectful of a culture that was completely alien to me. I had no way of verifying the truth of the information Oba was giving me about that culture. I was lost and disoriented in the gap between his world and mine.

I called Archer and told him the whole story. He thought I should just get out of it. I asked if he thought I should tell Miriam.

"No, it's better not to burn that bridge."

"What's sexual healing? Is it something any shaman would know how to do?"

"Sexual healing is to be able to have sex freely with no attachments and then go out in the world and see that Nature is the lover and the beloved in a constant state of orgasm. Being able to see and feel that constant orgasm is enlightenment. So sometimes the shaman might have sex with a woman to create that understanding, but whenever you are in ceremony, the shaman moves energy through the body. That energy is sexual energy, so it's natural to fall in love with the people you are in ceremony with. Everyone falls in love with the shaman. The natural relationship for men and women is for men to have many women and for women to have many men. The government and the church make the rule that you can only have one husband or wife to be sure children are supported and taken care of, but that's an artificial constraint. It's natural and good to fall in love. I think it's much better to fall in love than not to love at all."

"So I shouldn't hate myself for being stupid?"

"Not at all, but decide what you want your life to be like, and if you don't want this situation in it, let it go."

Oba called a few minutes later saying that he couldn't sleep because he thought I was mad at him. Miriam kept asking him what was wrong. She thought he was sick.

"What am I supposed to say? I'm upset because my girlfriend is mad at me?"

"You're supposed to say, 'I'm horny and I need sex. If you're not feeling sexual, we need to address this problem another way.'"

He laughed and said he'd try that. I told him what Archer said about sexual healing, and he agreed that ceremony brings up sexual energy.

"When you dress in white and cover your head with white cloth, you take the focus off the sexual." He admitted that he fell in love with everyone during ceremony.

On Arjuna's next visit, I initiated sex, but he didn't seem to be into it. On our post-coital pillow, he talked about home repairs.

"What's going on here? You certainly don't seem to be as interested in sex with me as you used to be."

"It's not you. It's just that sex outside my marriage doesn't seem so important now."

"Arjuna, maybe we've done the work that we needed to do

together, and we're just finished. If that's the case, let's own it and treat each other with love and support and not act like we don't find each other interesting anymore."

"That sounds right, and actually, you're more interesting to me than ever."

The next time Arjuna called, I told him I started my period after two months of not having one, "Sex with you must have kicked up my hormones."

"You need to have more sex. Why don't you just be flexible and get back in bed with Oba. You know you both want to. Just accept that he has other women, and he's afraid to tell you about it. I'm afraid to tell you the truth because I've seen you go ballistic when you're mad, and it scares me. It doesn't make any difference who else he's sleeping with if you're getting what you want."

Arjuna had conveniently forgotten the reason I went ballistic. I'd asked him to always use a condom. I provided the condom and handed it to him. Only after anal sex, did I realize he never put it on. Not only was ballistic an appropriate response, it was the only way to get him to take my boundaries seriously. It's because of Arjuna that I became an uber-vigilant condom cop.

I did think Arjuna was right that Oba was afraid to tell me about his other women. But why? I'd proved I wasn't jealous. Was he afraid I would reveal myself to them, and they would get angry? I had never revealed myself to Miriam or any of the others I suspected, so that fear seemed unreasonable to me. And if others "in the shade" did get angry and cut him off when they found out he had other liaisons, didn't that prove they were not good candidates for polygamy? Of course, I should have realized that Oba was simply a manipulative philanderer, but my confusion coupled with my addiction to our powerful sexual chemistry allowed me to keep myself in the dark.

August 1995

When my three-month hiatus ran out, Oba and I both wanted to go back to bed. We went to have HIV tests together, and we were both negative. After about three weeks of euphoric sex, Asante took me aside and told me she knew for sure that Oba was having sex with at least three other women besides me and that he approached another woman who refused him.

"You're in it with Miriam whether you like it or not. She's your sister. You have to deal with her."

I hated to hear it, but I knew Asante was right. I told Oba there would be no more sex until we could both be honest with Miriam about everything.

It made me sad. I cried for two weeks. Then I realized that he'd probably been having sex with other women without using condoms while trying to get away with not using condoms with me. We'd been conscientious about it, but only because I diligently patrolled that boundary. I got mad. He'd endangered my life, and I called him on it.

"Your life is very precious to me. I would never put you in danger. My medicine is so strong that I am completely protected. I cannot get any disease, and if, for some reason, you got sick, I could cure you."

Oba totally believed what he was saying. I wanted to believe him, but suddenly the culture gap got as wide as Grand Canyon. My powerful, magical healer was morphing into a dangerous, life-threatening monster. Modern science dueled with ancient wisdom. If he had a cure for AIDs, why hadn't he shared it with his suffering homeland? Thank God, I'd insisted we use condoms since he apparently felt no need to practice safe sex. Damn him!

He wasn't Shango. He was Eshu, hiding behind my head, pushing me toward self-sabotage. Of course, my conscious mind knew I should run far away from him as fast as I could, but my shadowy, addicted subconscious longed for the high communion of our bodies, for the ecstasy of sacred sex, for the joy of our divine connection. Part of me wanted to trust his magic, but I knew better than to bet my life on it. Oshun was riding me. Eshu was pushing me. The tension of opposing energies within me kept my mind and heart spinning. I was confused, dizzy and filled with fury, teetering on the edge of a chasm filled with lust, doubt and delusion.

A few days later, Asante called and told me she got caught in a hellstorm at Ifa Center. She went by to pick something up and heard this whole story from Miriam about how Yvonne told her about Oba's philandering. Asante said names were flying all over, and she wasn't sure how many women were involved or who was accused of what. I asked if my name came up.

"No, but it's a terrible mess. Miriam wants to blame everyone else. She wants to call all these women and tell them they can't come to Ifa Center anymore. Then Oba came back, and they started to fight."

I wondered why I wasn't a suspect. I thought Oba's affection for me was obvious, but I hadn't been around Ifa Center much in recent weeks. Maybe I seemed unlikely because when tempers flared, I played the level-headed peacemaker. However, with accusations flying, I might find myself in the line of fire.

Oba called late that afternoon. I said, "I heard you got caught with your hand in the cookie jar again."

"Yes, again."

According to him, he had been practicing with a new electric band for the premiere party of the movie he shot in Texas. When he chose the people to play the gig, Yvonne didn't make the cut, so she was mad at him. While he was out, she went to Miriam and told her that he had affairs with her, Bernadette and Devmata. Yvonne said she got pregnant and had to have an abortion. Miriam refused to believe Yvonne's story and insisted that she made it up because she was mad at Oba. Devmata denied everything, and Miriam believed her because they were "sisters." Oba told me Yvonne was lying.

"How could she get pregnant when she's not menstruating?"

"And how do you know she's not menstruating?"

"I overheard her tell Miriam once," he scrambled.

"She's anorexic. She stops menstruating when she's under-nourished. When you have sex with her, she feels better about herself and starts eating and starts menstruating again. The fact that you have sex with her makes her able to get pregnant."

Oba was doing that abusers' thing of getting all his victims to keep his secrets. I admired Yvonne's courage for speaking out and disrespected Oba for calling her a liar. I wanted to be as brave as she had been, but I was afraid that if I spoke out, he'd call me a liar too. Then I'd know for sure that I wasn't special to him. Although I called him on his shit, at that point, I, too, was a victim willing to keep his secrets.

The next morning Oba called to see how I was feeling. I told him I felt bad for Yvonne because it took a lot of courage for her to tell the truth, only to have him call her a liar.

"But you don't know how sick she is?"

"That doesn't matter. She came to you for healing, and you hurt her. Western psychotherapists know that the patient always falls in love with the therapist. They even have a word for it, 'transference.' That's why there are laws against psychiatrists having sex with their patients. In this case, you're the therapist, and you had sex with her. Of course she's in love with you."

"But these women know I'm married from the beginning."

"And they know you're not happy, and you're making love to them and telling them all those same things you tell me about how special they are."

"I don't tell them that."

I laughed. I realized that all this scandal had been a great test of my intuition. My instincts had been proven to be completely accurate.

I told Oba I would not come to any more ceremonies. He asked why not.

"I'm trying to avoid talking to Miriam, because if I talk to her, I'll feel like telling her about us, and I know you don't want me to. Besides hanging around makes me feel like I'm just one of your groupies."

"What's a groupie?"

"It's what the rock musicians call the women who hang around just to have sex with them."

"You're much more than that."

December 1995

After four months, I was jonesing for some drumming, dancing and *orisha* energy, so I went to Oba's full moon ceremony. None of the accused women were there except Devmata. As I was leaving, I saw Oba sit down on the sofa and Devmata kneel at his feet as though she was going to give him a foot massage—or a blow job. He looked uncomfortable, spotted me and jumped up to walk me out. A premonition flashed across my mind: *Within a month she'll be pregnant. Oba will continue romancing me saying, "You're the only one I ever fell in love with, but what can I do? Now I have to support two families."*

The next time Arjuna came to town, he told me that he'd decided to recommit to his marriage and be faithful to his wife. Later I heard through the grapevine that he'd hit on another woman in our spiritual circle within the week, and she rebuffed his advances. Later still, Asante revealed that he approached her around the same time. Although she was tempted, she resisted. Note to self: The man who asks you to keep his secrets keeps secrets from you, guaranteed.

So here was another gorgeous spiritual man, who had his own healing center, being dishonest about his pursuit of multiple sex partners. Why tell me a fictional story about recommitting to his marriage? Especially after he counseled me to just accept that Oba had multiple women? The excuse about being afraid I would get mad was bogus. I never asked for exclusivity or got angry about other partners. I only got mad when he penetrated me without the condom I provided, which in my eyes was a passive-aggressive rape and a dangerous deception.

Of course, Arjuna and Oba aren't the only spiritual leaders guilty of keeping sexual secrets. Revelations of child sexual abuse have rocked the Catholic Church. Evangelical Christian preachers, such as Jim Bakker and Jimmy Swaggart, fell from grace because of sexual scandals. Buddhist leaders Osel Tendzin, Richard Baker and Joshu Sasaki Roshi engaged in sexual misconduct. Amrit Desai, founder and leader of Kripalu Yoga Center, resigned after admitting to sexual intercourse with followers. Jewish spiritual renewal leader Marc Gafni continues to be dogged by multiple allegations of sexual misconduct. And the list goes on. Spiritual predators are deft at dodging accountability and often remain unapologetic, even when forced to relinquish power after being exposed. Spiritual communities seem to suffer from a special style of denial since they rarely have strategies in place to define and resolve such abuses.

Other powerful men—movie stars, politicians, billionaires— also philander, so perhaps we should just acknowledge that men drawn to leadership tend to have extraordinary libido and prefer multiple sex partners. Our culture's taboo against non-monogamous lifestyles pressures these men to lie about their behavior. Openness about this social-sexual phenomenon would be more authentic, responsible and life-affirming, but that may not be the point.

I think that deception itself is the thrill for Arjuna, Oba and probably many other men. Deception gives them control in a situation where they lose themselves in the communion of orgasm. Authenticity and intimacy are what they fear. To keep that fear at bay, they manipulate.

Manipulating their followers and all the women in their lives makes them feel powerful. Well, yeah. Manipulating makes anybody feel powerful, but spiritual teachings are supposed to help us learn not to do exactly that. You know, have faith! Trust the Universe. Let go, let God.

To me, spiritual leaders who are dishonest and deceptive are simply not practicing what they preach. It's hypocrisy, and under that hypocrisy I see deeply wounded men who lack the courage to accept responsibility for the consequences of their actions and do the healing work that could save their souls. They are frauds. Their abuse of women fills me with rage. Their woundedness makes me sad. Their pathetic cowardice inspires my contempt.

If I was truly honest, I would have to admit that part of the responsibility for their behavior lies with me. I spiritualized my own love and lust because they were healer/shamans. I was party to their deceptions. I defended their dishonesty. I wanted to be their special, spiritual one. My rage, sadness and contempt deserved to be directed toward me too.

This realization was only beginning to enter my consciousness as I was living that moment. I was still under Oshun's spell. By New Year's Eve, I was desperate for another fix of dance, drums and Oba's charisma. I went back to Ifa Center, where wild energy throbbed in the liminal night. Oba was stunning in dark maroon robes with white embroidery. During the ceremony, he used a live white hen to clean us of negativity, by holding the passive chicken by her feet and waving her around each person. Then somehow he hypnotized the bird and placed her on the altar where she sat quietly as we celebrated the I Wo San. We danced and danced and danced until three in the morning.

Afterwards, I asked Oba if the hen would be sacrificed. He said he would take her to a creek in Topanga Canyon and release her, "Oshun will handle the sacrifice." At that point, I should have realized that when a holy man can put a chicken about to be sacrificed into a trance and make it sit still on an altar for three hours, he can do the same thing to a woman, in fact all the women in his life, for years on end.

1996

Oba called on New Year's Day to say how beautiful I was the night before and how much he loved me. I asked him if Devmata had taken pity on him and offered to meet his sexual needs. He insisted he was not sleeping with her.

"Oba, my intuition tells me that you are and that she will be pregnant within a month. Be very careful about birth control."

Miriam called minutes later, unaware that Oba had called, thanking me for helping out. Then she initiated the conversation I'd been trying to avoid.

"I don't know if you've heard some of the awful rumors that have been going around lately."

"I've heard them. Just take them as a wake-up call that you and Oba need to work on your relationship. When it's off or stressed between you two, we all see it, and it's bad for Ifa Center. All any of us can do is work on ourselves."

It was completely crazy. I was advising my lover's wife on how to save her marriage. I felt compassion for her, but I couldn't figure out how to be compassionate. If I told her the truth, she'd hate me and blame me for ruining her life. If I didn't tell her the truth, I would have to live a lie and hate myself. I'd ended my affair with her husband, but I was still in a no-win situation.

January 23, 1996 – My 49th Birthday

Oba and Miriam gave me a book for my birthday, *Awo: Ifa and the Theology of Orisha Divination* by Awo Fa'Lokun Fatunmbi, and in it I recognized more similarities to the Native American teachings I'd been studying. Both systems use trance in healing. Both systems emphasize drumming, dance, meditation and fasting as paths to spiritual growth and healing. Both systems emphasize the constant transformation of energy into matter, intention into action. Both systems teach that we make an agreement before we are born about what lessons we want to learn during our life and what will happen to us that will allow us to learn those lessons.

When I told Oba about the similarities, he said, "Thank God. Now you see." I explained that, according to Native American teachings as I understood them, because of our pre-birth agreements, we were not allowed to complain about anything.

"Thank you! That's exactly right."

"But Miriam complains about everything all the time. Does that mean she doesn't really understand what the religion is about?"

"Yes. It does."

I noted Fatunmbi's version of the story of Shango: As a mortal man, Shango was a great warrior and dictatorial ruler. He was married to the beautiful and powerful Oya, who was previously married to Ogun. When Oya left Ogun, she took his sword, which she always carries with her to cut to the truth. She provided Shango with the tools to create thunder and lightning. Oya helped Shango plot to manipulate his two most powerful generals into a conflict so they would destroy each other. The plot went wrong, and one general emerged victorious and toppled Shango. Shango was driven into exile, and Oya followed him. Shango was so remorseful over his mistakes and previous dictatorial behavior, he hanged himself. When his followers heard of his death and rushed to claim his body, no body was found hanging there. In his act of remorse and contrition, Shango transcended the human condition to become the *orisha* Shango. When he hanged himself, Oya drowned herself in the Niger River and also transcended to *orisha*. Later Shango fell in love with Oshun and left Oya.

The great warrior abused his power but became divine after he took responsibility for what he did. Fatunmbi writes, "By incarnating Shango as *orisha*, the universe allows for transformation through tragedy and crisis. When those who are in a position of authority abuse their power, it can lead to disastrous results. When that same person learns the lessons of their own self-deception, they can often become strong forces for change."

After I read this passage to Oba, he admitted that his seductions were abusive. He confessed he slept with Bernadette, Devmata and me. He still denied Yvonne. Oba was living the archetypal drama as he wanted to live it, without atonement or taking responsibility for the consequences of his manipulations. In my view, by ignoring the key lesson, he was obstructing his own redemption.

At this point, I was still so arrogant and deluded I thought I could save him. Marsha, a white woman from Los Angeles, would show a Yoruba *babalawo* the true meaning of the mythology of his ancestors. My pure love would give him the courage to live the traditional way in the light. Together we would fearlessly live the truth of polygamy without hiding in the shadows. What was I thinking? As I look back, I'm embarrassed. Of course, he was a lying philanderer. But in my eyes, at that time, he was a stranger lost in a strange land, and I was the one who could lead him out of the wilderness.

I also knew that if I called him a liar in the face of his denials without proof, it would be easy for him to make me look like the crazy one, and I'd be dismissed as a jealous bitch. If I patiently questioned him and calmly stated my doubts, my anger would seem sane and justified when proof of his deception came to light.

Summer solstice – 1996

During Oba's spectacular summer solstice ceremony in Topanga Canyon, I noticed a coyote watching the action from the hill above us. Since coyote is the trickster in Native American mythology, I took it as an omen that something shadowy was going on that I couldn't see. After the ceremony, I stayed to clean up. Oba asked me to help him dismantle the Oshun altar. He instructed me to put the honey in the river and scatter the fruit along the bank. We hid behind the bushes and stole some kisses. I put the rose petals in the water, and we watched them float downstream. Some get stuck on the rocks. I asked him what that meant.

"It means that love is not flowing smoothly for us yet. We are stuck for now."

August 1996

Sidney decided to celebrate her 50th birthday party at a festive Caribbean restaurant, a women-only celebration. I mingled with women of different ages and races as bouncy reggae music played in the background. Asante motioned for me to sit beside her.

"I want to extend an invitation to you, but it might be sensitive."

I poured a glass of iced tea from a frosty pitcher.

"What is it?"

"A baby shower for Devmata."

I tore open a straw and jammed it into the tea.

"Devmata's pregnant?"

Asante's ornate golden earrings bobbed and sparkled as she nodded her head. I sipped the cold bitter tea and placed the glass on the garish orange, pink and yellow print tablecloth. I looked Asante in the eye.

"Is Oba the father?"

She looked back into my eyes.

"Yes."

I looked away and reached for the tea. The chill of the glass ran from my hand, up my arm to my heart. I could hear the laughter and carefree chatter of other women floating around me. I was envious of their easy, happy lives. Tears blurred my vision, but I willed them not to run down my cheeks. I took a big gulp of the cold tea, swallowed my anger at Oba and turned to Asante. I took a deep breath and tried to relax my throat so words would come out.

"I'd like to go. We need to welcome this child into the world."

My head spun. My heart pounded. I was amazed to hear myself say those words. Asante smiled a gentle, loving smile. Her white teeth blazed across her elegant ebony face.

"Good," she said. "I hoped you'd feel that way."

"Do you think Devmata would be willing to meet with me before then?"

Asante took my hand. It was cold and wet from gripping the glass of tea. "Yes," she assured me. Her touch warmed my icy hand. "I'll arrange it."

The baby was due September 18th. I recalled the coyote and the chicken laying an egg on the altar at the summer solstice ceremony. Devmata would have been six months pregnant by then. The baby was conceived in January. I remembered that I told Oba about my premonition and warned him to be careful about birth control on January 1st. I was furious that he'd been lying to me for eight months. Asante said he told Devmata that he told Miriam, but she refused to believe it. I doubted that he did. Asante felt that if he owned the situation and convinced Miriam to embrace Devmata as her sister, and the baby as David's sibling, Ifa Center could transform and move to a new level. I agreed and added that my relationship to Oba should come out of the shadow at the same time.

When I got home from the party, I finally let my tears fall. Of course, I didn't sleep all night. I just lay in bed exhausted as my brain boiled. Oba showed up at six in the morning. Although I wanted to tear him limb from limb when he walked through the door, I managed to remain calm.

"Remember your promise that you were going to tell me when you had sex with other women? Isn't there something you need to tell me now?"

"It's true. What you've heard is true."

He'd finally told me the truth, although only after I'd already discovered it from another source. His honesty didn't feel as good as I'd imagined. My intuition was vindicated. It had been right on all along, yet I wished it had been wrong. I told Oba he must put everything out in the open and get Miriam to accept Devmata as a sister and bring the baby into the house as David's brother. At the same time, he needed to tell them both about me. He said he knew I was right.

"You've abused me, Miriam, Devmata, Yvonne and Bernadette, and you need to own that in order to heal it. If you do, everyone can grow from this. There's more to religion than drumming and singing prayers. Religion is about how you live your life. If you do love me, you're dishonoring Oshun by keeping that love in the closet. You're dishonoring Yemoja by denying your child and its mother."

I got teary when I said, "I would have much rather found out from you than heard about it at a birthday party."

He said he was sorry. Then he tried to put the blame on Devmata.

"She was supposed to be using birth control, and she didn't. She didn't tell me in time to get an abortion."

"Don't waste your breath on excuses. The problem started with your choice. You know what a condom is and how to use it. You are not the victim in this situation. You are a powerful healer, and you agreed to all this before you came here. Now you've set up a really difficult challenge for yourself. Let's see you do your stuff. Heal yourself and all the women you've hurt."

"Can you forgive me?"

"Of course. As healers, forgiveness and compassion are the tools we work with. What form that forgiveness will take depends on what actions you take now. If you handle this in a way I can respect, I can forgive you completely."

"I didn't tell you because we have so little time together that I want it all to be happy time."

"Needing to be happy all the time is addiction. We need to be present with difficult emotions as well as joy. Otherwise, the joy is false."

When I told him I planned to meet with Devmata, I felt his heart stop.

"That really scares you."

"Yes, but it's OK. I know you have to."

Of course, this was exactly why he was lying to me all along. If I knew the truth, everyone would know the truth, and his tenuous empire would fall. To him, my honesty must have felt like betrayal. To me, his house of delicately balanced secrets was destined to tumble down anyway because it betrayed the spiritual truths that were supposed to be guiding our lives.

When Asante asked Devmata if she wanted to invite me to the shower, Devmata said that she had seen me and Oba kissing in the parking lot and felt I was her rival, but she'd changed her perspective since then. I told Asante that I felt Devmata and I could embrace each other as sisters, but Miriam would be a problem. Asante said, "Miriam is a problem, because she wants to be the boss."

I met Devmata for lunch. She was more together than I'd ever seen her. She told me she'd gotten off Prozac and marijuana. She'd been in therapy and was recovering from her obsessive-compulsive disorder. She said she'd accepted that Oba wasn't capable of being there for her. I didn't feel jealous of her at all, probably because I was so grateful that I was not in her position. If she was jealous of me, she didn't show it. In fact, our curiosity and eagerness to share information after years of secrecy overrode any competitiveness.

We compared notes without emotion. She started sleeping with Oba in April 1994. I first went to bed with him that September. He called us both almost every day, usually collect. He came to her late at night to avoid her 15-year-old daughter. She said she got pregnant January 15th at four in the morning, two weeks after I told him to be careful. He told us both he loved us, and if we would just wait, Miriam would accept us as a second wife, and "we will be one big family." She still saw him occasionally (which I assumed meant that they were still having sex). She asked what I'd do if I got pregnant too.

"I won't. I insist that he use condoms."

"You got him to use condoms? How'd you do that? He won't use them with me."

"I made it clear that there would be no sex without condoms. He doesn't like it. I have to remind him every time, but he uses them."

I asked her if he called her when he went to Texas to work on the movie.

"Every day, sometimes more than once a day."

"Me too."

We tried to figure out how many other lovers he'd had besides us. We listed me, Devmata, Bernadette, Yvonne, and probably two of the young dancers. I wondered how he scheduled them all. She thought he didn't sleep and maybe had more than one woman a day—morning, noon and night. She said she accepted that he would always have lots of women.

I told her I found him passionate and potent but uneducated on sexual technique, although he was getting better, "But you've studied Tantra. You must have a good sex life."

"To tell the truth, he's always so tired and stressed out, I haven't demanded much from him. He gets mad at himself when he comes too quickly, and I don't want to make that worse."

Finally, I asked Devmata, "Are you comfortable with both of us having a sexual relationship with him?"

"Absolutely. I've always believed in universal love. I think it would be an ideal thing to have a community where people shared all kinds of relationships with other people, including sexual ones."

Would I be comfortable with both of us having a sexual relationship with him? I didn't know, but I did feel a profound shift in the situation. At least Oba, Devmata and I had moved into a place of honesty with each other. Destiny was forcing Oba to take responsibility for his actions, so redemption seemed possible. I felt suspended between conventional morality and the myths of the *orishas* with their multiple loves, betrayals and dramas. I wondered if Ifa's mythology was a mirror of human nature, a new paradigm for non-monogamous bliss, or a template that perpetuated dysfunction and suffering. I decided I was willing to participate in a polygamous experiment.

Then Devmata told me things about Miriam that made my hair stand on end. When she started going to Ifa Center, Devmata was leaving a lover, had an ugly relationship with her ex-husband, was having trouble with her children and was looking for a sanctuary to escape her life. She said Oba was always sweet and loving to her and, although she felt she had a deep karmic connection to Miriam, Miriam was constantly abusive. Devmata wanted refuge in their house and gave or loaned them money to help them with their financial problems, including one loan of $3,000 that they never made payments on (although she said Oba recently started making payments without Miriam's knowledge). Devmata co-signed on a credit card for them, and they ran it up to the $2,500 limit and never made any payments.

She claimed she was telling Miriam all along that Oba was coming on to her and that she was attracted to him. She said she used to ask Miriam to walk her down to the car to protect her from having to be alone with Oba.

"She knew all along, but she basically let me buy her husband."

Devmata explained that when she was giving them money, Miriam would put Oba and Devmata together and then expect Devmata to cook, clean, sew and massage her. When Devmata would run out of money, Miriam would accuse her of trying to steal her husband and ban her from the house until she needed help or money, then she'd call Devmata again. Devmata said she thought Oba tried to pay her back with love and sex for all the money she contributed and all the abuse she took from Miriam.

If Devmata's stories were true, Oba and Miriam's behavior was even darker than I imagined. Were they grifters? Was Miriam Oba's pimp? How much was Devmata exaggerating to excuse her adultery? The shadows around me were so huge, I could not see my own.

A few days later, Oba and I were making beautiful love. We fell back into each other's arms as though we'd never been apart. My hurt and doubt disappeared as our bodies melted together in the highest sacred communion. I succumbed to my drug.

I was caught in Oshun's rushing river, and I couldn't see the treacherous waterfall just ahead.

Chapter 3

Shango's Fire

Devmata gave birth to Ashay on Yom Kippur, the Day of Atonement, 1996, which also happened to be the autumn equinox. Asante called to report that Oba had told Miriam everything. I felt relieved, like I'd been released from the prison of lies. Later Oba called and told me he and Miriam were fighting constantly, and she was physically attacking him.

October 1996

Miriam called, her voice stern and scolding as she asked me to tell her about my relationship with Oba. I took a deep breath and launched into our whole history, without pausing for her to comment. Finally, I stopped, barely breathing, and waited for her response.

"Oba told me he's only had sex with you twice."

"We've been lovers for two years."

Her voice pounded me like a sledgehammer.

"You're a heartless, home-wrecking snake!"

I stayed completely calm and grounded, so much so that I'm sure I came off as heartless. I didn't deny any accusation. I didn't defend myself.

"I knew all along you would get hurt, and I felt very conflicted about that. Several times I called off the sexual part of the relationship because of it."

"Can't you see how hurt I am by this?"

"Of course. That's a totally appropriate way for you to feel. Anything else would be denial. I betrayed you, but I don't consider myself a home-wrecker because I think you and Oba should stay together as parents and partners and work at having a better relationship."

"I can't have a better relationship with him if he's sleeping with you," she snapped. "Oba is sick. He has a sexual obsession."

"He could be addicted to sex," I concurred. "He's certainly addicted to marijuana."

"By giving him sex, you're enabling him to continue his addiction."

"If I stop giving him sex, he will go get it from someone else."

"I'd rather he have sex with someone that he didn't feel close to."

She was admitting she would turn a blind eye to his cheating, but she didn't want him to have an emotional connection to his lovers. Her definition of monogamy split some pretty fine hairs. I wondered if Oba knew he had her permission to have sex with strangers. She tried hard to get me to promise I'd stop having sex with him. The more she demanded, the more I resisted. Her refusal to take any responsibility for the situation triggered my "you're not the boss of me" reaction, so she went in for the kill.

"You're ruining David's life."

"What is David learning about loving relationships from observing you and Oba?"

"Oba and I have made a pact that he won't have sex with anyone else for six months," she announced imperiously, "and we will work on our relationship."

I wanted to laugh, but I didn't.

"He hasn't told me about it, but if that's what he wants, he won't be contacting me."

"Why didn't you tell me about it sooner? I've been trying to get people to tell me the truth for months," she said, donning the mantle of self-righteous victim.

"Linda told you the truth. Yvonne told you the truth. You called them both liars and threw them out of the house. I knew that if I told you the truth you wouldn't believe it. It had to come from Oba."

"I guess I wasn't ready to hear it."

"That's true," I answered gently, glad to see a glimmer of self-awareness.

Miriam returned to her victim role, ranting about how much she had done for Devmata before that snake stole her husband. She said she hoped Devmata would suffer and be unhappy. She went on about how she helped Devmata relate to her son (I'd seen Miriam be so abusive to Krishna that I was amazed Devmata didn't take him and walk out).

"Be careful about playing the Grand Victim," I warned. "When Devmata was in the house, she made a lot of important contributions, mainly financial. You had a definite give and take with her."

I expressed my concern that the lying and deceit gave Ifa Center a bad reputation and disgraced the name of Ifa. I told her I thought her desire to create a spiritual community expressed her highest self, and with this foundation of truth, the community could begin to heal and flourish.

"What we're doing right now is the practice of Ifa. We've called Eshu out from behind our heads so we can own our negativity and weaknesses. Now, Eshu will become our messenger to Spirit."

Miriam interrupted me in a scolding tone.

"You're so heartless. You don't even feel any remorse, and until you feel remorse, I can't forgive you."

"It's true that I don't feel like saying I'm sorry. What matters is how we heal ourselves so we don't make these mistakes again. We are all powerful healers—you, me, Oba, Devmata. We chose this path, so I can't feel sorry for myself, and I can't feel sorry for you. I'm just glad that we're getting on with our work."

"Well, I'm making this a healing experience for me."

She hung up, called Devmata and dumped on her. Devmata told Miriam she was sorry and hoped Miriam would forgive her someday. Miriam called me back ten minutes later.

"I asked Oba if he loved you or had some special relationship with you. He said he didn't love you, and he was just hustling you for sex. He really loves me. He wants to be here with me. He's just using you."

By now, my heart was pumping pure fury, but I managed to keep my voice calm.

"I think that's quite possible. Thank you for telling me. We're powerful when we tell each other the truth. Let's keep talking."

After I hung up, I allowed myself to feel hurt by Oba's spineless willingness to throw me under the bus.

Much later Oba called. His tense and constricted voice triggered my addiction. My fix was at hand. I forgot my anger and said, "Oh thank God. We must talk."

"I'm calling to tell you I'm no longer interested."

"Don't hang up. Please Oba we must talk to each other. She twists what we tell her to turn us against each other."

Miriam got on the other line and interrupted.

"I want all three of us to talk together so we know what was said."

"That's a good idea."

Miriam asked a rehearsed, rhetorical question.

"Oba, are you a polygamous man?"

"No."

I retorted.

"Then what have we been doing for the last two years?"

"Having fun."

"Oba, yesterday Miriam told me that you swore you wouldn't see another woman for six months..."

Miriam interrupted screeching.

"More than that! We're trying to get our marriage together!"

"So you don't want to see me anymore. Is that true?"

"Yes."

"She told me that you told her that you don't love me, and the whole time you were just hustling me for sex. Is that true?"

"Yes. I said that."

Miriam screeched again, "Two years? I thought it was only 10 months."

"We got together around his birthday shortly after his mother died. You can figure out the dates. It was from then until Linda told you about Bernadette. Then we stopped having sex until last April."

She screamed. He scrambled.

"It hasn't been that long."

I hung up. She called back.

"You're not my friend. You're not helping us! Stop meddling in our marriage. Oba doesn't love you. Get out of our lives. Leave us alone!"

"I'll be happy to."

I knew exactly where I stood. Oba was a liar and a predator who would never stick up for me. In fact, he was mad at me because I'd broken the unspoken code of silence of the dysfunctional family. If I'd been rational, I would have walked away forever. I didn't. Oshun tempted me with sweet self-deception. I couldn't resist.

By this point, I too had embraced and embodied the *orisha* archetypes. I put my ear in his soup, but contrary to the myth, Oba did not defend me against his vindictive wife. When the chips were down, he could not summon Shango's decisive strength. He chose her over me. Oba lived the core myths only when they told stories he wanted to live, and I did the same. Just as he resisted atonement and redemption, I resisted the sting of betrayal and deception, even though I recognized it in the mythology.

The day of the next ceremony, Miriam left a message on my voicemail, "Marsha, I just want to be sure you understand that it would not be a good idea for you to come to Ifa Center." I knew I couldn't expect her to embrace me after I'd betrayed her, but I saw why Oba had to lie to her. She punished everyone who told the truth if it was something she didn't want to hear. To be part of her spiritual community, you had to keep secrets and collude in her denial. There was a mandate for deceit, and it came directly from her.

Infidelity is a perfect storm of weaknesses. Miriam refused to consider that all the parties involved shared responsibility.

Oba called and reported that Miriam was hitting him and spitting on him. I wondered who abused who first. Who was the victim, and who was the abuser? To me, they both looked like abusers. From Miriam's point of view, maybe Oba deserved to be spat on. Was her behavior appropriate? Maybe, but neither one of them behaved like a healer or spiritual leader.

November 1996

Baba Olatunji came to town for a public concert. As a peace gesture, Oba offered to introduce me to the legendary musician. Oba sneaked me into the green room. Olatunji's entourage welcomed me. Oba spoke to Olatunji in Yoruba as he introduced me. As the old man took my hand, I said, "Oba has told me all about you—wonderful things. I'm very pleased to meet you." He had warm, wise energy. Afterwards, I asked Oba what he said to Olatunji.

"I told him, 'This is one of my wives.'"

December 1996

With the monkey of lust still on my back, I met Oba for lunch. He was contrite and apologized for saying he didn't love me, but at that moment he had to tell Miriam what she wanted to hear. I didn't understand or agree, so I took everything else he had to say with many grains of salt. He claimed things were better between them, everything was out in the open with Miriam, and they could talk about anything.

"Are you going to tell her you had lunch with me?"

"No."

"What will your life be like if everything turns out the way you want it to?"

"I'd have a polygamous family with three wives and several children, and we'd all work together."

"Could the wives have other lovers in the house, or would they have to just be with you?"

"Just with me."

"WHY?!"

"OK, you could."

"Would all the wives know about each other?"

"Absolutely!"

"Would you also have secret girlfriends?"

"No, everyone would know who I'm with."

"Would we all live together?"

"In Africa, if they can afford it, they have a big compound where everyone has their own room, but all the rooms open out onto a central common. That might not work here, and we'll have to adjust by having separate households."

"Is polygamy part of Ifa or just a cultural custom?"

"Some people want to be monogamous, and that's OK. Some people need to be polygamous, and that's OK. Polygamy becomes part of the religion when it's necessary to have more than two *orisha* energies to make the family function successfully. You might need to put Oshun and Oya and Yemoja together to have a balanced unit."

"What would happen if Miriam didn't come around to this way of thinking? Would you leave her and have a family with just me and Devmata?

"No. Once you have a child with someone, the three of you are a unit that's *awo*."

He explained that *awo* was usually translated as "secret" but "mysterious" may be closer to the meaning. There's no precise English equivalent, but it refers to the hidden principles that explain the mystery of creation and evolution. *Awo* is the esoteric understanding of the invisible forces in Nature which remain awesome and elusive and can only be grasped through direct participation. Anything that can be known by intellect alone ceases to be *awo*. He was in *awo* with Devmata and Ashay as well as Miriam and David.

"Are you in *awo* with me too?"

"Yes."

"Why? We don't have a child."

"I don't know, but I know we are."

He added that if he determined that Miriam wouldn't come around and couldn't handle the truth, he could go back to having secret wives.

"Where does that leave me?"

"It's up to you to decide if you want to be with me without letting Miriam know."

I said that I thought his vision of a happy polygamous family was a fantasy. In reality, Miriam would be terribly jealous of the other wives and make everyone miserable.

"What happens in Africa if one wife is jealous of all the others?"

"It happens all the time. That's what all the ceremonies and divining and sacrifices are about, to make everyone get along better."

"How do they handle day-to-day life if everyone is fighting?"

"She stays on her side of the compound, and you stay on yours. It's not uncommon for one wife to take revenge on the other's children."

"I wouldn't trust Miriam with Ashay."

"I don't think Miriam will go that far, but it's something I'm considering. When I grew up in the royal household, the rule was that children were only allowed to eat at their parents' house or their grandmother's house to protect them from poisoning by the rival wives."

"So polygamy does not make women happy. The husband must manage all these different, incompatible personalities."

"Yes. That's what life is, finding ways to get along."

"If I'm one of the wives, and I decide I want to maintain a separate residence on my own dime, would that be allowed?"

"Yes, of course. That's your choice."

He said sometimes the wives get along like sisters, and you can't tell who is the mother of which child because they all love all the children.

"That was how it was with my father's wives."

I told him I was softening my position on needing to tell Miriam the truth. I said I thought it was important that we did tell her the truth, because we gave her a chance to take responsibility for her part in the situation, and she didn't take advantage of it. Oba said hiding things from her equated to everyone staying on their own side of the compound. Miriam was already in a polygamous marriage whether she liked it or not.

After lunch, we went over to Devmata's so I could take some pictures of the baby with his parents. It was the first time the three of us were together since our polygamous relationship was outed. Devmata and I both noticed Oba's discomfort with the situation, although he started to relax when he saw that we were friendly with each other. When he left, he embraced each of us separately and tenderly. Dealing with the nuts and bolts of polygamy was new for him too.

1997

I was an April fool, deaf to the hollow sound of my own excuses. As blossoms unfolded, I welcomed Oba back into my bed. I knew I was addicted to sex with him, but doesn't Nature intend us to get addicted to sex? How else would life go on?

On a balmy spring morning, we made love gloriously, passionately, joyfully. It was hot and sweaty. We moved in perfect slippery rhythm. Afterwards I said, "That's God."

"Yes."

"Some people never have sex that good. We are rich people in bed."

"Yes, and just think, right now most people are at work pushing pencils. We are like rich people making love all day."

We lay quietly for a while, then he looked at me and said softly, "If I've done anyone wrong, it's you." I kissed him and said, "I forgive you."

In the afterglow, Oba said he knew I must have other men.

"You're so beautiful. I can't imagine that all the men who see you don't want you."

"So you don't want me to tell you about the other men?"

He jumped. I said, "Just kidding." We laughed. I asked him to explain what was going on for him when he was bedding multiple women simultaneously.

"I just thought if they were interested, I shouldn't pass it up," he smiled with disarming charm. It was the most honest answer he'd ever given me, and it was exactly how I felt about Arjuna.

Since I had no way of knowing if Oba was a reliable informant, I was always looking for outside sources. I discovered a Yoruba community's newsletter devoted to polygamy. I showed the publication to Oba and pointed out that it said that the African man always financially supported all his wives.

"When are you going to start paying my rent?"

"That's when he's a rich man. When he's living from hand-to-mouth, he's supposed to give her moral support."

"I'm only getting five minutes of moral support a week, and it's not enough."

I wrote a letter to the publisher, an Ifa priestess named Funmilayo. I described our situation and asked how she thought the teachings of Ifa should be applied to heal it. Funmilayo called me when she got my letter and said she didn't know where to start answering my questions. She opposed polygamy. She said it was not part of the religion, but it was definitely part of the culture.

"It sounds like all the men do it."

"They do."

She felt polygamy worked entirely to men's advantage. She was raised in a polygamous family and said that the trouble was that it was always like what we were going through. Wives argue with each other because the man seems to like one better, or gives a nicer gift to one's child, or spends too much time with one. She said women in Nigeria are brainwashed to accept it, but they are unhappy at least half the time. She thought women shouldn't fight each other because men are the common enemy.

According to her, the husband must tell the first wife before he takes a second wife.

"Of course, the first wife is always hurt and angry."

She faulted Oba for not following that rule because honesty is part of the religion. She said a father must support all his children completely. He didn't necessarily have to support the wife, but he usually gave her a place to live and helped with big expenses.

"If you can't pay your rent, you have no business getting involved in polygamy."

As I suspected, Oba was trying to get away with murder in the culture gap. The information that polygamy was always just like what we were going through slapped me upside the head. Like it or not, I was in a polygamous relationship. I didn't like it.

Funmilayo made it clear that she thought the problem really began with Oba lying to his first wife.

"You knew he was married. He didn't lie to you about that."

"Yes, I'm not innocent. Is it traditional for the first wife to have the power to control the whole situation?"

"Believe me, the man has complete control. He's doing exactly what he wants to do."

Although I was careful not to name names, the local Yoruba community was small, so Funmilayo knew who my letter was about and faxed a copy to Oba and Miriam. Miriam went ballistic. Oba got mad at me for "causing trouble." Apparently he'd been telling Miriam that he was not having any contact with me or Devmata, but the letter proved otherwise.

"Your letter opened a wound that was almost healed!"

"So you plan to keep me and Devmata and the baby in the closet forever? That's the best we can hope for?"

He tried to deny it, but he was trapped.

"I'm just trying to keep peace."

"Avoiding conflict isn't keeping peace because it doesn't solve problems. You're asking us to keep your secrets to make your life easier, but you don't care about what problems it creates for us."

"What kind of problems do you have?"

"The baby doesn't see his father. Devmata is trying to raise a child alone, and I never get to see my lover. Those are problems."

I went to meet with Funmilayo. She described how vicious polygamy gets in Africa.

"The favorite wife and her children may become a target for the other wives. Sometimes her children are poisoned. The other wives will gang up on the favorite wife and have a spell put on her or kill her, so they can have more attention. I refuse to practice polygamy because it's dangerous for women and children. In my experience, polygamy doesn't work in Africa or anywhere else. It didn't even work for Fela Kuti. He divorced all his wives, and now he's dead from AIDS. Most of those wives will probably die of it too."

Like most Africans, Oba had idolized the charismatic Kuti. Although Oba lacked Kuti's courage for speaking truth to power, I suspected he'd adopted his countryman's devotion to music, love of smoking weed, trick of twisting the tradition of polygamy to suit his personal purposes, and belief that the *orishas* would protect him from the HIV virus. Both men were blind to their hubris. Oba never commented on Kuti's death and its concomitant revelation of tragic flaws.

I realized that, as enlightened as I thought I was, I was behaving like one of the jealous wives. I decided to exit the polygamy soap opera. When Oba called, I told him I was taking myself out of the relationship. He said he understood although he didn't agree. I told him what Funmilayo said about the viciousness in polygamy. He pointed out that jealousy occurs between the siblings of monogamous families too. He felt it was just the way people were, not the fault of polygamy or monogamy. He may have been right about that, but certainly multiple sexual partners made jealousy more potent and relationships more complicated.

I asked him to recite the words of one of his songs.

"The people you love, you know like the touch of their fingertips. The people who love you, you will never know."

Then he translated the second verse, which I hadn't heard before.

"We are only speaking this way now because we are angry."

We wished each other well.

Oba called a few days later.

"Devmata told me that you think she should sue me for child support."

"She asked me if I thought she should sue you, and we talked about it. I said I didn't think she'd be able to get much money."

"She said it was all your idea."

"I'm hearing that you're looking for someone to blame for the problem you created. The problem is not what I said or Devmata said. The real problem is that you got Devmata pregnant, and now you're legally responsible for supporting that child. You need to take responsibility for solving that problem."

"I'm just telling you what Devmata said so you'll know she talks about you behind your back."

"Listen, if you're asking whether I think you should be providing financial support for the child, the answer is yes."

He weaseled off the phone. I wondered if Nigerian wives were always fighting because their husbands played them off against each other. Maybe the concept of manipulation is inherent in Ifa. Certainly *ebo* cultivates favorable energies, thus manipulating life. Yet the other indigenous religions and shamanic practices I'd studied frown on manipulation because it indicates a lack of trust in the wisdom of life itself. I'd learned that the only thing we can control is our response to what life deals us, but Oba tried to control other people. Did Ifa diverge philosophically from other indigenous religions, or was Oba violating Ifa principles, or was Oba exploiting cultural difference? As I pondered this, I tried to figure out how to get Oba to change. Slowly, the irony of my own manipulations began to dawn on me.

I talked to Devmata later. He called her right after our conversation and told her not to talk to me. I told her she had to stand up to him. Having two wives stick together and support each other was new for him, and he really didn't like us having that power.

The next morning, I woke up feeling a strong premonition that some tragedy would happen when Ashay was in Oba's care. I hoped my intuition was wrong.

A few days later, Devmata called and told me how much she appreciated my support and admired me for having the courage to speak the truth. Then she did an about face and sweetly told me she didn't want me to talk to her about Oba or my relationship with him. She said it was too painful, and she wasn't ready for universal love. I agreed to honor her request, assured her that I was no longer involved with Oba, but pointed out that not sharing information about our relationships with Oba gave him all the power and allowed us to stay in denial.

"I understand your point, but I just can't handle it. You have a lot of freedom, and I don't have any. I don't want to hear about your freedom because that's painful too."

In the course of one brief conversation, she went from telling me how much she appreciated my support to how I wasn't supportive at all. She hoped to win Oba's favor by following his orders. In the process, she gave him the means to deceive us both.

Oba was right all along. Everyone wanted to be deceived. Of course the truth was painful, but unless his women found the courage to compare stories, he controlled everything with his lies. I was secretly relieved that Devmata didn't want to play the polygamy game. She and Miriam were not women I would choose as my sisters. I felt free.

1998

Common sense and healthy rational choices proved to be no match for the cravings of my heart and the appetites of my body. In February, I fell off the celibacy wagon into Oba's open arms once again. As always, when he was with me, he was attentive and adorable, as though I was the only woman in the world. In that moment, he was absolutely sincere, and I'm sure he was similarly sincere with other women in other moments.

I told him I thought I'd come to a better understanding of his rules, sort of "don't ask, don't tell." He said that was almost it, but Yoruba culture also allowed the man to collect wives that would bring him material or social benefits, in addition to the wife of his heart, and all the wives were supposed to get along together. He said he had offended me the most and I was the wife of his heart.

"You're the one I love first."

Of course, he was smart enough to know that each wife wanted to be the wife of his heart. Managing his harem would become easier if we all believed that he loved us first. In his culture, women were currency to be collected. I was not providing him any material benefits. My own finances were in distress. However, since I was in the entertainment industry, he may have seen my connections as a potential social benefit.

1999

On my birthday, January 23rd, Oba woke me up with a phone call at one in the morning. Within minutes, he was in my bed making love to me. It was a cold night, and his body was hot. He was literally generating heat, the perfect birthday gift.

On Valentine's Day, he showed up at midnight wearing a sparkly, red-striped hat covered with hearts. My Valentine! He was so darling. We fell into bed. He treated me to two orgasms. He'd mastered the skills and was able to last a long time. We both enjoyed the deep sensuality of every part of the lovemaking.

I would let Oba know when I heard rumors that he was pursuing other women. He didn't deny them. Sometimes he gave me advance warning about upcoming scandals. We settled into cautious intimacy. When he was with me, I felt special, and in the face of overwhelming evidence to the contrary, I held onto hope that he would change, leave his wife, stop philandering and appreciate the devotion of his true spiritual partner: Me! I was suffering delusion induced by the drug of lust and my own need to feel lovable. Since Miriam had banned me from ceremonies, I was in withdrawal from the ecstasy of the dance and the intoxicating rhythm of the drums.

One afternoon, after an argument followed by a sweet, sweaty session of make-up sex, Oba said he had to go get a goat for a ceremony and asked if I'd like to go with him. I'd set myself up for this by telling him that I was interested in learning more about the sacrifices and ceremonies. Make no mistake. I'd never taken animal sacrifice lightly, but I'd also questioned animal rights activists' emotional condemnations without any investigation into the spiritual rationale behind such rituals. In Nature, animals kill and eat each other. We are animals too. Ritual sanctifies this natural behavior and shows respect for the animal's gift to us. Indigenous hunters seek to embody the unique intelligence of their animal prey through dance and rhythm before the hunt and by consuming the meat with respect and gratitude.

When Oba was one of a few experts booked on a TV talk show supposedly investigating voodoo, an animal-rights activist asked, "Do you make your children watch the murders of terrified, innocent animals?"

Luisah Teish, powerful, articulate, outspoken author, story-teller and priestess of Ifa, said, "I'd like to answer that. The murders your children see on TV are much more destructive than what my children learn when they are involved in a sacred ritual that connects them to their place in the food chain."

Wade Davis, author of *The Serpent and the Rainbow*, added, "If you really care about the slaughter of innocent animals, why aren't you picketing Kentucky Fried Chicken?"

In ancient times, Hebrews, Greeks, Romans, Celts, Aztecs and Mayans all sacrificed animals. Today, the practice continues in Judaism, Hinduism, Islam and traditional African religions. The New Testament refers to the parents of Jesus sacrificing two doves (Luke 2:24).

Wholesale condemnation of animal sacrifice implies that we believe death is bad or to be feared. Death is part of the cycle of life. All living beings experience death eventually. Will we be terrified at the moment of death? Or is courage as natural as death itself?

As I agreed to go with Oba, I had a vision of a live goat tied up in the backseat of his car, shitting all over the carpet and the upholstery. I asked him how we were going to bring the goat back in the car. He said the goat would be sacrificed at a farm in San Bernardino because it was illegal to slaughter goats within Los Angeles city limits. He'd already done all the prayers and incantations at home. In this case, the goat would be eaten by the family and friends of the client, so the goat could be killed in advance.

We drove the smoggy freeways, stopping at a big box store to buy a square plastic tub, a screw-top plastic jar, and a bunch of big plastic trash bags. We drove past pungent dairy farms between green fields. We turned down a narrow rural road and pulled into a small farm behind a white cottage. Cattle, pigs, sheep and goats were confined to separate pens. Some donkeys grazed next door. A parked ice cream truck played a jingly tune. Hispanic and Asian workers in blood-splattered yellow rubber aprons and rubber rain boots casually sucked on Popsicles. They all knew Oba and greeted him warmly. He told a small Mayan man that he needed a goat.

As we walked to the goat pen, we passed three black and white calves lying on the ground with their legs tied together. The pen teemed with 40 or 50 goats. Oba perused them, pointed into the middle of the herd and said, "I want that one." I couldn't tell which one he was pointing to.

"Which one? The black one?"

"No, that one."

The Mayan man, another Hispanic guy and a Mexican woman jumped in the corral and seemed to know what he was talking about. They tried to grab a goat, and all the goats bolted and ran. The herd milled and churned inside the corral. Oba pointed in a new direction.

"He's over here! No, now here!"

I was still saying, "Which one?"

After running around in circles for a few minutes, the Mayan man grabbed a shaggy, spotted, white male by the horns and asked, "This one?" Oba said, "Yes!" They dragged the goat out of the corral by its horns. It squealed and dug in its hooves. They commented on its strength. Oba said that was what he wanted. They tied the goat to a railing where it banged against the wall and got tangled up in the rope. I felt sorry for it. It was a beautiful, strong male whose life was about to end. The Mayan man asked Oba if he wanted to cut its throat himself.

"No, you can do it this time."

Oba paid cash for the goat, $120.

We took the plastic tub, jar and trash bags into a cinderblock building adjacent to the corrals. On the way in, we passed two young Asian men loading pig carcasses (heads and skin on, beautifully cleaned of hair) into a pickup truck, maybe 10, as many as the truck would hold.

In a stark anteroom, more employees in bloody yellow rubber aprons and boots sat around eating ice cream bars. Flies swarmed everywhere. It smelled like blood and death. Through swinging doors, I saw animals being slaughtered and butchered in the main room. I stayed in the anteroom while Oba took his things into the killing room. He came back and said we had to wait for our turn. We went outside and bought drinks from the ice cream truck. I asked if he was going to sing prayers for the goat before they killed it. He said he already did that at home, but he had to catch the first blood from its throat in the jar for the ceremony.

"Maybe I'll stay in the car."

He said OK. He told me more about how the ceremony worked. The goat was thanked for giving up his life and asked to take the problems of the person being healed into the next world with him along with prayers to Oludumare from the people seeking help. The Mayan man came to get the goat. I decided that I shouldn't wimp out. I should observe everything for my own education.

As I followed Oba into the slaughterhouse, an employee dragged a struggling calf inside. I opted to watch through the swinging doors. Other people were inside watching, including an entire Hispanic family with two little girls. They were focused on a huge black bull that seemed to belong to them.

The Mayan man cut the goat's throat. Blood gushed out. Oba knelt and caught the foamy, thick blood in the jar. The goat was still alive. When the jar was almost full, Oba pulled it away and the Mayan man decapitated the goat with one strong cut. He threw the head onto a metal table. The goat's body continued to struggle, writhe and kick on the bloody floor.

"Oba, you got a strong one."

"That's why I picked him."

I heard a loud "crack" and turned to see the bull being electrocuted with some kind of big stun gun. The huge beast dropped to the ground, writhing and kicking spasmodically. A worker attached one of its hind legs to a chain/pulley contraption that hoisted the beautiful behemoth up to hang from the ceiling. The entire family stood at quiet attention, filled with respect for this majestic animal. A worker cut its throat and blood drained into a bucket. Gratitude for the bull's gift of life flowed from each member of the silent family.

The goat's body finally stopped thrashing and was hoisted up too.

Oba saw me watching through the door and motioned me inside with him. I figured if a seven-year-old girl could watch the slaughter of a bull, I ought to be able to handle the goat. I went inside and stood next to Oba. A young Hispanic man butchered the goat. First, he cut off the feet and placed the hooves on the table next to the head. Then he carefully skinned and removed the testicles, which were odd, oblong shapes with a flat surface on one of the narrow ends, slick and white like ceramic. The testicles were also carefully placed on the table by the head. Next, he carefully stripped off the skin. Oba would use this to make a drumhead, so he'd asked for a worker he knew did a careful job. This took some time, but when it was done, Oba stepped up with a plastic trash bag and the worker dropped it inside. I gave myself the job of pulling trash bags out of the box and handing them to Oba as needed.

In the meantime, the bull had been decapitated and was being skinned. Several pigs were electrocuted, squealing and twitching horribly, then blasted with a blow torch before having their hair scraped off.

The goat was split down his belly and chest. Goat guts and organs spilled out, all connected to each other, in various pastel shades of grey, white, pink, pale blue. The innards were dumped in a bucket that a female employee took to a sink where she carefully cleaned and washed them.

Another calf was dragged in. Its throat was cut while still

alive, like the goat. Blood pumped out on the floor before the calf was quickly and efficiently decapitated. Its body continued to writhe, but not as violently as the goat's. The goat was quartered, and its legs, shoulders and ribs cut into pieces on Oba's instructions by a table saw. All these pieces went into plastic bags. Oba carefully packed all the bags into the big plastic tub. Finally, he took the head and had them cut off the horns and split the skull laterally. He placed the hooves, horns, skull and testicles into the last bag. The cleaned intestines were delivered to us in a dripping, clear plastic bag. No one, workers, other observers or customers, seemed to have any problem with the unusual nature of Oba's requests. We loaded the goat into the trunk. By now, it was six o'clock, and we started back to L.A.

The scene had been horrifying, intense and unpleasant, but I didn't have a strong emotional reaction to it. Watching the goat sacrifice forced me to own my place in the chain of life and death, to embrace the part of me that is willing to kill to live. Oba and I talked about death and dying in the car on the way home. I asked when he thought the animal was actually dead, since the goat was conscious during the throat slitting and the body was still writhing after decapitation. He said he thought that as soon as the spinal cord was severed, the pain was gone, and the animal just went to sleep.

I reflected on the death of my parents. He listened and talked about the heightened psychic powers of elder people who are getting ready to die. I thanked him for bringing me with him.

"It was profound."

"Yes. It's important for you to understand where that meat in the market comes from."

But it was more than that. It was a day of experiencing life deeply by being present for sex and death. This was why I loved Oba so much. Other men might take me to dinner and a movie and sweetly tell me that I was just like Julia Roberts. Oba would make me angry, make wild love to me and then invite me to stare death in the face. He could be an exasperating child, but he had gravitas that took me close to the bone of life. I marveled at the paradox of how proximity to death made me feel alive.

Ironically, as we drove home, we were stuck in gridlock for a couple of hours because a meat-packing truck had spilled its contents all over the freeway. That evening, I sat in a trendy restaurant talking about the movie business with attractive young professionals, hoping no one would ask me what I did that day. Fortunately, no one did.

Throughout the summer, my frustration escalated as Oba repeatedly stood me up, failed to call, made excuses about dealing with crises in his other two households and found precious little time for me. When he made a date with me for a certain time, didn't show up for hours and didn't call, I was tormented by worry. I imagined that he was in bed with another woman or killed in a car crash. The infidelity scenario was likely, but the possibility of an auto accident was quite probable. Oba had minor scrapes due to falling asleep at the wheel more than once. He was always driving while stoned and sleep-deprived. His car was an old clunker that often broke down. When he would finally show up in the wee hours, I'd be so relieved that he was alive that I'd accept his unlikely excuses without question. When I felt angry because he didn't seem to value me, I'd ask myself: So is the joy he brings you worth all the pain he causes you? Sometimes I felt like it wasn't, but after great sex, the answer was, Oh yeah!

To quote a gay man friend:

"When you've got that good penis at home, you're blind."

Around the autumn equinox, I met Antonio, a dark-skinned, muscular immigrant from Mexico, with long, raven-black hair. Although he spoke very little English, I felt a spark. He asked if I was divorced. I said I was and asked him if he was.

"Almost."

He belonged to an Aztec dance troupe and taught me the

names of Aztec gods and goddesses including the goddess of butterflies and the goddess of adultery. I told him I had another man who came over sometimes.

"Do you love him?"

"He's married, and so are you."

"Not really."

As we got to know each other, he told me soldiers broke both his knees when he was a political activist over 20 years ago. Within a month, he was sharing my bed. Antonio was a wonderful lover with natural talent in bed. He was deeply sensuous and gorgeous, with a smooth, nearly hairless torso. He stayed all night, and I appreciated not feeling abandoned after sex.

As I looked at his beautiful body in the morning light, I noticed some scars on his wrists.

"This is where the soldiers cut me and put in the electric wires to send electricity through my body."

"When they broke your knees?"

"Yes."

He'd been fighting in the mountains and was captured. They took him to a military camp, broke his knees, electroshocked him and held his head under water.

"Why didn't they kill you?"

"My father had connections and bribed someone to get me released. I was 19."

After he got out of the hospital, he went back to the mountains and fought some more. He told me he wanted to go back to Mexico and fight with the Zapatistas.

The next night, Oba slipped into my bed at midnight. Before we made love, I told him I'd been seeing another lover. He didn't ask for details.

Sex with two different men on consecutive nights challenged all my good-girl training, but I decided "so what." Why did it have to be wrong? I had no intention of marrying or having children with either one. In fact, I felt empowered. When I told Sidney about Antonio, she said, "So now you're double fucking?"

"Yeah, and I'm enjoying it."

Antonio admitted that he was fighting depression. He'd separated from his wife only six months before. I worried that it was too soon for him to be getting involved. He insisted our relationship wasn't stressful, but he was worried about "getting his feathers."

In the Aztec dance troupe, before dancers could get their elaborate feathered costumes and perform, they had to learn choreography for four dances. Antonio was frustrated because he was still working on the third dance. He was worried because the materials for the costume would cost about $300, which he didn't have, and he was required to see his costume in a dream before he was allowed to design it. He felt like he'd never get his feathers.

After we'd make love, he'd sleep soundly, but one night, I could tell by his rapid breathing that he was dreaming. He called out, and I thought he might have been calling my name, so I answered. He went back to sleep. In the morning, he said he'd had strange dreams. I asked him to tell me about them.

"I was in your house, but it had three stories. You were climbing up to the top story, and I couldn't keep up with you, so I called out for you to wait."

Then he was in a swimming pool with big waves, struggling to swim. He felt he was drowning. He went down to the lowest level of my house, where he was all alone. He wondered where everybody was and went looking for people. Finally, he was dancing on top of a mountain.

"Were you alone or with your group?"

"Alone."

"Were you in your feathers?"

"Yes!"

"You dreamed your costume!"

While I made breakfast, he sketched his costume. I was flattered that he dreamed it in my bed, and I knew his dream meant that our relationship was doomed.

Antonio didn't call for days, but Oba did. He was more sweet and loving than he'd been in months. He said he threw shells for me and the divination was, "The balls of the goat are dangling, but they don't fall off."

"What the hell does that mean?"

"Things only look bad, but they're actually fine."

"Maybe I just need to have two men."

"No!"

"Why not? You have more than one woman. Why can't I have more than one man?"

"Because I say so!"

We both burst out laughing because his words sounded so ridiculous.

2000

As the millennium dawned, a golden Aztec warrior glittered in my living room. Antonio's costume was spectacular, gold and black and metallic blue with a fringe of golden beads. I told him he was *guerrero de oro*. We put the pheasant and peacock feathers into his headdress. The plumes did their own dance, bobbing and waving as he moved.

Antonio was becoming increasingly undependable and stood me up a couple of times. Just like Oba, he forced me into the role of condom police. I was in the same conundrum, just with a different guy. Whatever my issue, I knew I hadn't worked it out yet.

Four days before Valentine's Day, Antonio told me he didn't have time to see me and needed time for himself. I wasn't devastated, and I appreciated his forthright communication. I'd known ever since his dream of drowning that he wasn't ready for another intimate emotional relationship.

My relationship with Oba soon fell into the same old pattern. He stood me up, rarely called and generally neglected me. My neighbor told me Antonio had cut off communication with everyone in his family. In one sense, that news was a relief. He was withdrawing from everybody, not just me. On the other hand, I knew it meant he was in the grip of depression.

At the same time, my financial life, which had been precarious for some time, went from bad to worse. Film production work dried up, and I'd lost the desire and physical stamina to work the brutally long hours it demanded. I was deeply in debt and could no longer afford the payments on my house.

In mid-April, I decided to put my house on the market. By the end of the first week in May, I'd accepted an offer on the house for the full asking price plus seller's fees. I scrambled to find a place to live.

Oba called after a long silence and said he'd been busy fighting with Miriam. He wanted me to move close to him. He swore he'd find more time for me if I was conveniently located. Still under Oshun's spell, I looked at some apartments in his neighborhood. All I could afford was a cement box opening on a parking lot without a blade of grass for blocks.

The next morning, friends who lived in Mexico called out of the blue. I told them I was selling my house and didn't know where I'd go.

"Maybe I'll leave the country like you did."

"Why not?"

They offered to let me stay with them while I got settled in the charming village of Ajijic.

Did I want to live in a cement box and struggle to pay the rent to be able to have secret sex with Oba, with no hope that he would ever change? Or did I want to go to a gorgeous house in Mexico where I could write my book sitting by an aqua pool under a lavender umbrella with servants taking care of me?

Duh! I chose Mexico!

Antonio heard from his brother that I was selling the house and moving to Mexico. He came over to give me a Spanish lesson. We moved the lesson to the bedroom.

Oba finally showed about one in the morning of my last night in the house. We made love. It was good but bittersweet. My parting words were, "Thank you for everything. I still want to dance with you in Lagos."

I stayed in Mexico nearly five months, housesitting for various rich gringos, writing my book, teaching English at the local orphanage and visiting the Huichol people in their homeland in the Sierra Madre Mountains.

In November, my computer crashed a couple of weeks before my tourist visa expired, and I went back to L.A. Oba invited me to spend Christmas with him because Miriam was going be in Florida. I waited for him to pick me up, but he didn't show or even call. Four days later, he called with a lame excuse. I was furious. The grip of my addiction was broken, or so I believed.

2001

In January, I left traffic and smog behind and headed for Santa Fe, New Mexico. I drove across the gorgeous snow-dusted desert and arrived on an icy Saturday night. I began a new life in the New Year, new century, new millennium. I'd visited Santa Fe regularly. Its vast sky and artistic temperament had captured my heart. Santa Fe also boasted a vital African drum and dance community. A white woman named Liz taught 50 or more dancers three times a week. Although the drumming made me think about Oba, I was happy to be back in rhythm. Oba called once in March and made a half-hearted effort to persuade me to go back to L.A.

Antonio called in April. He was drunk, a shame because he'd been sober for some years. He said he was working all the time to support his family and had to give up Aztec dance.

After six months, I returned to L.A. for a visit and was immediately overwhelmed by the traffic, congestion and a brown soup of smog. I agreed to meet Antonio. He was drunk. He told me he loved me (which he never said sober). I told him I loved him, but I didn't want to be with him if he chose to be a drunk. He was such a gorgeous guy, a good man with heart who cared about his children and worked really hard. I was sure he suffered PTSD from the trauma of torture. I told him to call his Aztec teacher.

"I don't need him. I have you," clearly inviting me to be his enabling codependent.

I suggested he go to AA, but I knew he wouldn't. I saw so much sadness and pain in his face, with flashes of anger, but he wouldn't talk about what was hurting him. He let me know he wanted sex.

"Not when you're drunk. It's your choice—beer or me."

I left him falling-down drunk at the bus stop. It broke my heart to watch the bitter aftermath of torture destroy his soul, but I understood that I could not save an alcoholic. His addiction meant that our relationship was doomed to be dysfunctional. I recognized my codependence. I knew I had to set a boundary and enforce it, and I did. Why didn't I do the same with Oba? Although he deceived me with his duplicity and intentional confusion around cultural difference, I should have recognized an abusive situation. Had the African sorcerer made me his zombie?

September 11th, 2001 found me at my friend Carol Wilson's rustic bed and breakfast in a peaceful ghost town in southern New Mexico. Carol and I watched flickering images of airplanes crashing into the World Trade Center. The Millennium Apocalypse began while I was deep in serene wilderness. A couple of days later, I felt such strong concern for Oba that I couldn't resist giving him a call. He answered. I asked simply,

"How are you?"

"I'm fine. Everyone here is OK."

He ended the conversation quickly. I didn't speak to him until three months later when I was in L.A. for the holidays, and he left me a message. The number he called from was not Ifa Center. I called him back. He asked why I didn't call him if I was in L.A.

"You haven't called me in three months, so I assume you've found another woman and are finished with me."

"Not true. I lost your number and just found it yesterday."

"Where are you? This isn't the Ifa Center number."

"You mean you don't know?"

"Know what? I haven't talked to you in three months."

"Ifa Center burned down. We lost everything."

"When?"

"September 3rd."

He never mentioned it when we talked a couple of days after September 11th. He didn't remember my call. He told me the fire started in the back room, burned all their sound equipment, most of his drums and all his religious artifacts.

"Where are you living?"

"Miriam rented a place, but I'm living with Nigerian friends."

"You separated?"

"Yes."

"Are you getting divorced?"

"I don't know."

"When Shango burns down the house, it's a message to change your life and start over."

"I know."

Once I'd accepted that things would never change, everything changed! When I'd completely let him go, he separated from his wife. I hardly slept that night. Various Oba scenarios ran through my head. I asked myself if being with him was what I really wanted. I didn't know the answer, but I was willing to explore the question. Oshun tempted me again.

We made love. After months apart, we slid right back into it, laughing and caressing, our bodies fitting together perfectly. He stayed all night. It was wonderful to be able to cuddle with him, to know he was getting enough sleep and was safe. In the morning, I told him about New Mexico. He was interested.

The next time I saw him, he showed up about six hours late — in a brand new car! He said he finally had enough of his old car breaking down. He made a chunk of money on a gig, went to a car dealer, put $1000 down and got the car. It was even properly insured, more evidence that he'd really changed.

We made more love. His libido was remarkable for a man of 62. It was what kept drawing me back to him when I should have known better. My husband's libido was what held me in my marriage much too long. Apparently my own libido was exceptional because I had difficulty finding men who could keep up with me. When I did, I put up with far more bullshit than I should have.

Chapter 4

Wandering

I got a housesitting job near the beach in Venice. Oba loved the place and started staying overnight twice a week. I had always insisted that I would never let myself get in Miriam's position of managing his business, but as our emotional intimacy deepened, that resolve weakened. I suggested we take a road to trip to Santa Fe to explore teaching opportunities there. For me, the trip was an acid test. If it worked out well, I'd consider managing him and trying to build a life together. Oba agreed to the adventure.

Oba fell in love with Santa Fe. The adobe architecture and high desert climate reminded him of northern Nigeria. We went to a party where we meet more Nigerians, including a young master drummer named Ajaka, Katunga, a sweet teddy bear of a guy, and Kori, a gorgeous hunk with long cowry-flecked locks. These young men bowed to Oba and invited him to join their drum circle. Although Ajaka seemed to be at the top of the local drumming hierarchy, everyone treated Oba like he was the leader. Ajaka suggested that he and Oba work together and invited us to rehearse with him the next day. He cooked an African dinner for us that night and asked Oba to perform with him the night before we were scheduled to return to L.A. Oba was delighted with his newfound community.

True to his word, Ajaka booked a couple of gigs with Oba for late November. Ajaka suggested that I set up some workshops so Oba could make more money to cover travel expenses. I made it clear to Oba that I considered the venture an experiment.

When it was time to go to our first workshop, Oba wasn't ready. I started ordering him around to get him there on time. He pouted and said, "If I'm late, I'm late. So what?" I could see our whole relationship going the way of his relationship with Miriam.

"Oba, you complain about not making enough money, but if you want to make money in America, you have to play by the rules of business, and that means being on time. When you're late, you seem unprofessional, and because I'm in business with you, it makes me look unprofessional. If I'd known that your attitude was 'If I'm late, I'm late,' I would never have gone into business with you. But I have, and now I can't get out of it. For this tour, please make a point of being on time for me. If you don't want to do it after this, we won't do business together any more, and that will be OK."

He agreed. We were on time for everything. When we finished the tour, I said I thought we got along well except for that one argument.

"It wasn't an argument. It was just you forcing me to confront my shadow. And you were right. If I want to make money, I have to be on time."

Just when I was ready to write him off as a petulant little boy, he transformed into a responsible, self-aware man with whom I wanted to share my life.

2003

Our relationship became comfortable, sweet, loving and sexy. Oba seemed to have settled into monogamy with me. In April, while we were touring New Mexico, Oba got word that Baba Olatunji died. He was deluged with phone calls about memorial services and burial arrangements. I saw Oba as Olatunji's obvious successor in interpreting Yoruba music for Western audiences, yet I wondered if he had the ambition required to step into those shoes.

As we traveled, miracles were common. In Truth or Consequences (yes, that's really a town in southern New Mexico), Oba taught a small drum class in the blistering heat of a public park. A young man walked up and listened. Oba gave him sticks and put him on the djun djun. It was the first time he'd ever played, and he did well. Later that afternoon, Oba led an Oshun ceremony on the bank of the Rio Grande River. The owner of the property, a former Peace Corps volunteer in Africa, introduced us to his wife, who was in a wheelchair suffering from MS. Backpackers gathered for the ceremony. The young man who played djun djun joined the group. People brought offerings. Oba built an altar. After the first song, Oba turned to the group.

"The *orishas* tell me that some of the people here are dealing with loss. I'm supposed to let you know that whatever you've lost will come back to you, not right away and not in the same form, but that it will come back."

Then he continued calling in the directions and chanting to Oshun. He told everyone to put their offerings in the river with whatever intention they wanted to bring into their lives. We all danced and sang. The woman in the wheelchair stood up and danced with a big gourd rattle. Then she asked her husband to take her down to the river. She got in the water and prayed.

Then the young man approached Oba in tears. He told us that he'd been a prodigy Christian preacher. His young wife was the love of his life. Everything with her was blissful until she died in his arms of a diabetic coma nine months after they were married. His grief made him question God. He gave up preaching and had lived with depression for the four years since her death. He couldn't sleep at night and only slept during the day. That morning, he woke up to an inner voice telling him to go to the park, where he found Oba drumming. He felt what Oba said about loss seemed to be directed at him. The ceremony was a healing that lifted his depression. Oba told him to take his offering to the river and talk to the river as if it were his wife. He did. He came back weeping.

To heal a broken heart, go to the river (or flowing fresh water like a creek). Take honey and yellow flowers (yellow rose petals are best). Tell

Oshun you brought these gifts for her and put them in the river. Talk to the river exactly as if it was your former lover. Tell her everything you need to say. Listen for her response. You can ask her questions. Listen for answers. Allow yourself to fully feel whatever emotion comes up. When you feel complete, express your gratitude to your lover for all the good things you experienced together. Wash your hands and face in the river. Thank Oshun for washing away your hurt and bitterness. Say "goodbye" and leave.

As we toured, our relationship became effortless, and our love-making energized us. I felt so confident that Oba was faithful to me that sometimes I allowed unprotected sex.

By mid-December, we were exhausted. Constant loading drums into the car, unloading them into the venue and loading them back into the car became tedious. I felt overworked. We fought when I asked Oba to pitch in. He felt criticized and insisted he was working just as hard as I was. Glaucoma was beginning to compromise his vision.

2004

Devmata called me out of the blue. She said she realized she'd told me that she didn't want to know what was going on with me and Oba, but she'd changed her mind. She wanted to be included, along with Ashay, in the workshops and events Oba and I did together. She apologized profusely. I said it was unnecessary.

"It's OK to not want to be included, and it's OK to change your mind. It's OK with me if you and Ashay want to come to our events."

She said she wanted to go along on our next tour. I told her that wouldn't work. She offered to meet us somewhere and pay her own way. I told her that we moved fast, and it would be hard for her and Ashay to keep up. I pointed out that Oba wouldn't have much time to spend with them. This tour would include a Master Camp at Carol's bed and breakfast in southern New

Mexico. I told Devmata that would be the best possibility. She immediately bought train tickets to New Mexico for herself, Ashay and her mother.

In Santa Fe, Oba and I were embraced by Ajaka, Katunga and Kori. Ajaka's friend Henriette was visiting from Nigeria with her 13-month-old baby, Buki. Henriette called Oba "Baba" and me "Mom." Buki watched me with big, soulful, brown eyes—a little wary of this alien white woman. Much laughing, teasing and affectionate sparring in Yoruba made me feel the warmth of belonging to a clan. It was almost like having a family.

We traveled on to our Master Camp. Devmata arrived with her mother and Ashay. I hadn't seen Devmata for seven years. She was overweight with dyed red hair and bad skin. She talked loudly and incessantly. Devmata's mother was pleasant enough but elderly and frail. I hadn't seen Ashay since he was a baby. Now he was a darling eight-year-old boy—tall, dark, thin with a big smile like his father. He was independent and basically took care of himself. Ashay and I forged a friendly relationship. We played Frisbee and talked about the glorious New Mexico scenery. He seemed to trust me. When I observed father and son together, Ashay acted like Oba's "mini-me."

Devmata was a challenge. She took medication for bi-polar disorder and hadn't taken it during the train trip. At first, she was euphoric and emotional, gushing about how wonderful everything was, repeating herself over and over. Devmata told all our students that she was Oba's wife and I was her sister. (The wife part caused some confusion early on because Carol thought it was Miriam who'd booked the room). She wanted to take care of people and kept offering them things but refused to take no for an answer when they didn't want whatever she was trying to give. She couldn't pull herself together in time for class and only occasionally showed up for the last 15 minutes.

She, Ashay and her mother were never up early enough for breakfast with the other guests, so Devmata would start preparing food for herself or Ashay or her mother, then get distracted and walk away from it. Soon she'd start a different meal and do the same thing until there were six or seven uncooked, uneaten meals in different stages of preparation all over the communal kitchen. Finally, she'd completely lose focus and walk away leaving all the mess for other people to clean up.

Everyone was tolerant and compassionate, but I was afraid her behavior spoiled the experience of the other paying guests. Carol had the same fear and said, "Marsha, you know she can never be invited to anything ever again." I said I knew, but I hadn't breached the topic with Oba. He was patient and tolerant with her. If I expressed any exasperation, he simply said, "She's sick." Finally, I commented to Oba that polygamy could only work for me if I could choose the other wives, and I wouldn't choose a wife who was so sick.

2005

Oba suffered from a hernia in his groin since I'd known him. This problem caused fluid to collect in his testicles so they swelled to impressive size. His condition had worsened to the point that he was uncomfortable. Since he was still married to Miriam, and she was insisting that she was the only legitimate wife, I felt like she should handle this medical situation, but either she hadn't noticed or she didn't care. I researched *pro bono* healthcare options and took Oba to various free clinic appointments. Since his problem was not life-threatening, he waited weeks for treatment. Finally, Los Angeles County General Hospital scheduled surgery in late January. I took him to the hospital and settled into the waiting room. After a couple of hours, a nurse took me to the recovery room. Oba was groggy and disoriented. His balls were literally bleeding. I sat by his bed and comforted him as he came out of his stupor.

A nurse came in and said, "Your wife is downstairs and wants to know if she can come up to see you." We looked at each other in disbelief. Miriam had never shown any interest in this problem. I was surprised she even knew where Oba was.

"Yes. Tell her to come up."

We waited for her to appear. She didn't show, but Oba's cellphone rang. It was Miriam. I could hear her caustic voice from my bedside seat. She scolded him for having surgery without her. She played the martyr who was always left out. She cried crocodile tears about his infidelity with me. She ripped into him for all his failures as a husband. His pain was all about her. He listened silently. Finally, he said, "Sorry" and hung up. The man was bleeding and barely conscious. She never asked about his condition or the success of the surgery. She simply attacked him. No wonder he looked for love from other women. The fact that she never showed up made me think she wasn't in the hospital. She played her whole little drama from the comfort of her home.

After our August full moon ceremony at a yoga studio, one of the drumming students hung around and chatted with Oba after everyone else had left. She was a plain, 50ish woman named Jane, who was an M.D. When she finally left, I said to Oba, "She wants to sleep with you."

"I know. Don't worry. I'm on top of it."

"On top of it? Are you having sex with her?"

"No, of course not."

The familiar knot in my stomach told me he was lying.

My friends from Ajijic moved to Puerto Vallarta and built a Modernist house near the beach. They invited me and Oba to visit them in late November. I sprang for the plane tickets. It would be a romantic holiday for us. I'd traveled all over Mexico, but I'd never been to Puerto Vallarta because I thought it would be too touristy. What was I thinking? It was gorgeous, perched on a spectacular, shimmering blue bay. Yemoja at her most seductive was embraced by jungle-covered mountains. The quaint, cobble-stone-street town meandered up the hills. Cafe tables sat on the sand just steps from the ocean, under palm-thatched *palapas*.

Balmy breezes caressed us. The new house was sleek and minimalist. A garden lush with coconut palms and jungle flowers softened the stark architecture. It was a block from an empty, sugary beach.

It was a joy to travel with Oba because everyone wanted to talk to this exotic character. We met lots of people and made good connections. The first night, our hosts took us to an upscale restaurant where Oba jammed with local musicians. People got up and danced. The kitchen help pounded on every possible percussive surface. He got a huge ovation. The next night, our hosts had a party, and Oba provided the entertainment. Everyone had a blast and some of the guests booked private drum lessons.

The next day, as we walked on the *malecon*, we heard drumming. We followed the sound and found two young Mexican guys with a *djun djun* and a *djembe*. We introduced ourselves. Another *djun djun* player showed up, then another. They explained that young Mexicans interested in African music converge in PV during the high season to play for tips from tourists. They invited us to their rehearsal, and Oba gave them a free lesson. We had arrived on Monday. On Thursday, Oba found his band. By Friday, he performed with them in a public venue. They were so respectful, enthusiastic—and good! Of course, they had no money to pay for lessons, but I thought they could be whipped into shape and get gigs in bars and hotels, of which there were hundreds. They begged Oba to come back and teach them. I loved their sincerity and saw this serendipity as an omen that PV was where we were meant to be. Oba said he loved it because it reminded him of Africa—but less crowded.

On Saturday night, we went on a romantic dinner cruise. We drank Margaritas as we took a boat to a private beach. Mysterious shadows danced on rustic cobblestone paths lit with torches. We were seated for dinner at a table for two on the sand, just steps from the surf with the jungle behind us. We drank wine, then climbed stone steps to a buffet and carried our food back to the table. By the time we got to desert, I'd had lots of alcohol. As I was negotiating the uneven stairs with coffee in one hand and dessert in the other, I lost my footing and fell into the sand. I bumped a knee and twisted my ankle. I was terribly embarrassed by my undignified pratfall, which took the romance out of the evening for sure.

The next morning, my knee was sore, my ankle was swollen and I had a huge bruise on my butt. According to Archer, a physical fall must precede a major change in our psychological patterns. Since I fell while I was with Oba, I knew it meant that the pattern of our relationship would soon change. But how? The fall did not feel good. I suspected I was in for a rude awakening.

2006

In mid-January, Oba and I attended a conference where he presented a Shango manifestation ceremony on the first full moon of the New Year. In this fire ritual, participants released what they no longer needed and set intention for what they wanted to manifest. After the opening chants, we wrote down what we were ready to release on slips of paper and burned them. I wrote "struggle and rejection." After we tasted the flavors of life, we wrote down what we wanted to manifest, put money with it to energize it, danced up and deposited it in a big gourd. I wrote, "Get my book published." Later, Oba would give all these slips of paper to the ocean. Of course, we danced into deep trance.

The next morning, I read from my still-unpublished book as one of the presenters. Afterwards, one of the attendees approached me and offered to refer my book to his publisher. Shango's power was undeniable. He'd granted my petition within hours.

Oba and I went on tour again in March. In Sedona, Oba smoked a lot of pot with his student Charles, a big lovable guy who was enthusiastic about Oba's teaching. By the time we got to Santa Fe, Oba had a bad respiratory infection. Oba called Miriam and got a prescription for an antibiotic from her. I was puzzled and asked how she could have that.

"She had it for herself and is giving it to me."

We met Ajaka's new wife, Shandi, recently arrived from Nigeria. She announced that she was expecting. Since she hardly showed, I was amazed that the baby was due any day. After a Friday night show, Ajaka took her to the hospital, and she delivered a baby girl. Mother and child came home the next day. Oba was still feeling bad and wanted to go to bed early. Ajaka wanted us to celebrate with Shandi and the baby. I called Ajaka to tell him that Oba was already asleep, and we'd come the next morning. Ajaka insisted that I get Oba up and bring him over for a little while because "it's tradition." When we got there, we joined other Nigerian men including Katunga, Kori and Tookay, an amazing performer on bata, a type of drum associated with the thunder of Shango. Shandi was up and serving guests. She looked almost completely slim.

The men were so happy about a new baby in the house that they were drumming, singing, dancing, drinking beer and eating hot pepper soup with every part of the goat (which was supposed to help the father get his virility back). Occasionally, Tookay just had to jump up and dance a little jig for joy. I was touched by this celebration. Nobody had ever seemed very happy about babies in my family. I said to Shandi, "The men are so happy, you'd think they did all the work." She laughed and said Ajaka was so tired he was sleeping as much as the baby. The baby slept through everything.

Ajaka asked Oba to do a naming ceremony for the baby the next weekend. In Yoruba culture, babies don't have a name for the first week, then they get lots of names that have all kinds of auspicious meanings. We were to pay for the privilege of giving the baby a name, and our cash gifts would go for newborn expenses.

About 8:30 a.m. on Saturday, we went over to Ajaka's. Of course, they were just getting up. Oba sent me out to get fruit, flowers, candles, white bowls—all the supplies to build an altar and do the I Wo San. Twenty or more people showed up. Oba got all the guests to help cut up bitter kola and tease the tiny alligator pepper seeds out of bumpy brown pods that look like the rough skin of their namesake. Oba did a great job of leading the ceremony, blessing the baby's names and getting people to put money down on the altar to give her even more names. I experienced the Nigerian custom of "spraying" for the first time. The mother danced with the baby while celebrants put paper money on her head or on the baby. The money fell on the floor. The other children picked it up and put it on the altar. Oba coached me to get lots of one dollar bills for the occasion. It was fun. I felt like I was in Nigeria.

By the time we got back to Sedona, Oba was exhausted and sick. He and Charles smoked more weed and drank Guinness. Charles insisted Oba go to his drum circle. It was outdoors, and the night was really cold. Oba was cranky and short with me. I offered to break up with him. He insisted that he didn't want to end our relationship. The next morning, his respiratory infection was much worse.

Four days after we got back to L.A., Oba called to tell me he was in the Emergency Room at Cedars-Sinai Hospital. He was in unbearable pain and so unsteady on his feet, he couldn't walk. Miriam took him, and they were checking him in for a couple of days of tests and observations. I visited Oba the next day and had to leave to avoid crossing paths with Miriam. The good news was he didn't have a heart attack or stroke, no brain tumor or cancer, but he had Guillain-Barre syndrome, a temporary inflammation of nerves that causes paralysis. The cause is unknown except it follows a viral infection. It goes away by itself, after two months' rest. Of course, he went back to performing as soon as he was discharged.

The next month, Oba's life became a litany of calamities. His son David was in a serious auto accident, suffered major head trauma and needed brain surgery. The accident was a week before an important workshop that Oba and Miriam taught annually at a Big Sur spiritual center. I assumed they would cancel, which would hurt them financially, but to my surprise, Oba and Miriam went to the workshop and left David in the care of friends. Miriam may have been a harridan, but she was a devoted mother. I found it odd that she would leave her son, especially during surgery. Before he left, Oba fell down some stairs and injured his knee. Fortunately, David made a full recovery.

When he returned, I took Oba to pre-op appointments for his own surgery to relieve his glaucoma, since again Miriam showed no interest in his medical problem. When it was time for me to take him to the hospital, he was missing in action. When I finally got him on the phone, he told me that Miriam decided she would take him to the hospital and care for him after the surgery. I went nuts. I screamed at him about how he was abusive to me. He said he was sorry, but he'd promised Miriam.

"But you also promised me. Why do you feel like you have to keep your word to her, but not to me?"

"Because she'll get angry, and you won't."

"Not this time! Fuck you, Oba!"

I hung up, then called back and left a message for him.

"Oba, I will meet you at the hospital. Tell Miriam that during this crisis, you want your whole family with you. I am just as much a part of your family as she and David, so I am coming to the hospital."

I found Oba alone in the waiting room. She never intended to stay with him at all. She just didn't want me there.

That night, I dreamed that Oba was doing something shady and hiding it from me.

A few days later, I met Oba to advance him money for eye medication that he couldn't afford. While we were having lunch, he got a phone call.

"Hi, Sweetie!" he answered, "I'll call you back later."

"Who's that?"

"The landlady from my church."

"Is she your sweetie?"

"No, I call everybody that. She always calls me 'Honey,' and says she loves me."

"Oba, you have another girlfriend."

He denied it.

After lunch, we sat in my car and talked. Oba looked tired. I asked if he'd lost interest in sex with me. He said he hadn't felt up to it since being sick. He said he had desire, but his body didn't have the strength. With his injured leg, he didn't think he could find a position that wasn't painful. I said I understood, but I missed sex and missed him.

I asked if he was keeping secrets from me.

"I don't always tell you everything that's going on with Miriam and David and Devmata and Ashay just because it's too complicated and unpleasant."

"If you have another woman at the church that you want to be with more than me, you should be with her. I will move on without getting mad. You should be with who you want to be with."

"If I'm going to get involved with another woman, it won't be someone at the church."

He assured me that he didn't have the time or energy for another woman and that he deeply appreciated me. We did have sex one afternoon, gingerly working around his injured knee, and it was good. He confessed he'd been avoiding sex because he was afraid it would leave him feeling weak, and yet his protestations of low libido did not reconcile with his fine, rock-hard erection.

We'd shot an instructional DVD during Master Camp, and I

wanted to have it ready to sell for our next tour. One of Oba's students, a graphic designer, volunteered to create the cover. We set up a photo shoot on Saturday afternoon before his regular class. I asked Oba to spend the night with me Friday, so we could go together (and I could be sure he got there on time), but he said he couldn't because he had to go to church that morning. The graphic designer and I arrived on time. Oba showed up late with Dr. Jane in his car. When she stepped out of the car, I asked her, "Did you go to church?" She looked confused. I took Oba aside.

"Did you spend the night with her?"

He denied it and accused me of being jealous. He said he asked her to take a look at the medications Ashay had been prescribed at school. Dr. Jane seemed nice, but I noticed her sallow complexion, limp hair and sunken heart chakra.

"You know, for a doctor, she doesn't look very good."

He laughed and said, "I know."

She watched quietly during the photo session. After the photos were finished, we talked while we waited for Oba's class to start. She knew lots of information about his medical condition that hadn't been shared with me. I was glad to get the details, but I felt like I'd been left out of important communication. And how did she get the information? I could tell my conversation with Dr. Jane was making Oba uncomfortable.

Devmata asked Oba if Ashay could go on tour with us. I said it was fine with me. In fact, I'd suggested it some time ago. Ashay needed to get away from his mother, and I enjoyed his company. In Santa Fe, he'd have fun with the other Nigerian kids and learn social skills.

Chapter 5

Thunder of Truth

July 2006

The day before we left for our tour to Santa Fe and Sedona, Oba was running behind schedule as usual. He asked me to help Ashay pack and load his things in the car. When I arrived, I overheard Ashay talking to Jane on the phone. Devmata thought he was talking to Oba. As I packed Ashay's things, I gently talked him into going with me. I told him he and Oba would stay at my place that night, and we would leave in the morning. Ashay felt nervous about being away from his mother, so I chatted with him in the car. He told me he'd been on sleepovers before... to Jane's house.

"When you spend the night with Jane, where do you sleep?"

"I sleep with Oso."

"Is that her dog?"

"Yes."

"Is your Dad there?"

"Yes."

"Where does he sleep?"

"With Jane."

My heart stopped, but I took a deep breath and continued casually.

"How many times have you slept over at Jane's?"

"Maybe five or six."

"For a long time or just recently?"

"It's kind of new. Maybe a few weeks."

"When your Dad stays with you and your Mom, where does he sleep?"

"He doesn't stay with us."

After I got Ashay settled at my house, I felt like calling Jane, but what should I say? Now I was in Miriam's position. I tried to call Oba, but of course, his voicemail was full. By 11 p.m., I was able to leave a message that Ashay and I were expecting him. He called back and said he couldn't come because he had to do his ceremonies for the trip. I asked him to talk to Ashay. He told his son he'd meet us around seven the next morning.

At 11 p.m., I decided to call Jane. Her voicemail answered.

"You've reached Jane and Oba." Then Oba picked up.

"Guess who this is?"

Silence.

"Ashay told me that you're sleeping with Jane, and from her voicemail, it sounds like you're living with her. I'm really disappointed that you haven't been honest with me about this."

Silence.

"I would like to talk to Jane."

"All right. Hold on."

Jane came on the line.

"Hi Jane, it's Marsha. You know that Oba and I are lovers, right?"

Silence.

"Now I know that you and Oba are lovers too. I'm not particularly surprised because he comes from a polygamous culture. I understand that, but I don't like lying. My deal with him is simply that he always be honest with me. I've asked him directly a couple of times if he had a relationship with you, and he denied it. I want you to know that you can be honest with me, and I want Oba to be with who he wants to be with."

"I don't know what to say."

"Has he been honest with you?"

"Not about being lovers with you."

"Yeah, we've been lovers for about 10 years. This started in a situation where he was with a lot of women and lying to all of us. Obviously, I knew he was married to Miriam, and when we were honest with her, she didn't handle it very well. Oba and I worked through that, and I think there was a period of monogamy, until he started up with you. I want to handle it better than Miriam did, and I think if we are honest with each other, we have more power in this situation."

"I agree that we need to be honest, and I have no anger toward you."

"You know we are supposed to go to Santa Fe tomorrow, right?"

"Yes."

"At this point, I think we should go to Santa Fe and have the best time we can. Then sit down and sort this out when we get back."

"OK, and it sounds like you two have a lot to sort out yourselves."

"Yeah. Can I talk to Oba again?"

She went to get him. The line went dead. I called back, and he answered.

"Ashay misses his mother. He's being really brave, but it would be best for him if you were here tonight. If you're not here just because you want to have sex with Jane one more time before you go away for two weeks, you should make a sacrifice and stay with us."

"I will be there after I do my ceremony."

I was shaky and nauseous. I wanted to cry. I waited for Ashay to fall asleep before I let my tears fall.

Oba didn't show up all night. In the morning, I helped Ashay shower and dress. He kept asking about his dad.

"He will be here soon."

Oba finally showed up about nine. Oba and I went outside to talk while Ashay played video games.

"Anything you want to say?"

"Sorry."

He came up with a bunch of excuses about how sick he'd been and how "so many things happen to me."

"But I'm always here for you, to listen and help and make love. I'm not Miriam, I'm not critical or abusive, and I ask you for nothing."

"That's true, but sometimes you scare me."

"What are you afraid of?"

He couldn't articulate it. Perhaps he was afraid because I called him on his shit; or because I was a loose cannon. Indeed, I'd just exploded his world of deception.

I asked what went on with Jane. He said they fought all night, and she wanted to break it off. I told him I would not go to Santa Fe with him. He could go with Ashay and stay with Ajaka, or he could cancel the whole trip. Of course, he told me things would change.

"Does that mean you will give up Jane?"

"I can't promise that if you really don't want me to lie."

"So how will it change?"

"I will start giving you more time."

"If you are not giving up Jane, how could that be possible? It just doesn't work from a time management standpoint."

"You'll see."

He begged me to go to Santa Fe with him.

"Why? I'm just going to be sad and miserable the whole time."

"No, you won't. I'm going to treat you like a queen."

And, although I knew better than to believe him, I tossed my ear into that big pot of soup yet again. I agreed to go. I wanted the fun of the music. I wanted the adventure of travel. I knew the relationship couldn't survive, but I wanted some kind of graceful closure. After all, it had been a 12-year relationship. Looking back, I laugh at my silly excuses.

Under my fury at being deceived about Dr. Jane, I felt a quiet relief because part of me wanted to be on my own again. I wanted out of taking care of him, dealing with the unpaid phone bills, the lost cellphones, the nights he didn't show up, the stories that didn't make sense, the serious marijuana addiction, endless excuses, medications he couldn't afford that went on my credit card. I didn't want to see his eyes cloud up, his teeth fall out, his legs collapse under him, his body in constant pain.

In my eyes, Oba was a rock star, a rogue and rounder for sure, but a wild magician who glittered in every spotlight. As his companion, I shined in his reflected brilliance. His attention made me special. Although I was in my 50s, I felt like a sexy teenager every time I got to say, "I'm with the band." Part of me wanted that magic to last forever. Another part of me saw that Oba's charisma was fading fast. If I didn't want to see his spiritual power sputter and die, I needed to slip his grasp.

As we drove off to Santa Fe in my car, tension crackled between us. I interrogated Oba about the affair with Jane. Ashay seemed content and relaxed as he played video games in the back seat. On the way, Oba broke a tooth while eating cashews. The exposed nerve punished him with pain.

The morning after we arrived, Oba was agitated after he called Jane, and she told him she was packing up his things. The next morning, she told him to stop calling her. I took pleasure in this, although I didn't express it. Oba insisted that everything had happened for a spiritual purpose.

"Now Spirit is speaking to us. We can't know now how this will benefit us in the end."

I agreed, "You are acting as Eshu to teach all of us through reversal. I will grow from this. Jane will too. Hopefully, you will too."

"You have Eshu in you too."

I acknowledged that was true.

A dentist put in a temporary filling that relieved Oba's immediate pain. I put $250 on my credit card and told Oba I wanted to be paid back out of the proceeds of the drum workshops. That night we taught a workshop. Oba felt better. We began to feel more comfortable and forgiving toward each other.

The next morning, Oba's cellphone wouldn't work because he hadn't paid the bill. He used my phone to check his messages and discovered that Devmata had been trying to call Ashay. He used my phone to call her so they could talk. When Ashay finished, I took the phone and talked to Devmata. I told her that I'd found out about Jane. She said, "That's very painful." She took a little delight in the fact that it looked like Jane would throw Oba out. Devmata proceeded to tell me that she and Oba had a sexual relationship until a year ago when Miriam called and screamed at her, "Are you having sex with my husband?!!" Devmata decided to be celibate at that point. She admitted to lapses a couple of times before Oba's surgeries when he came over and begged because it "might be the last time." She said he was angry when she stopped having sex with him and would still come over and try to talk her into it occasionally. I felt betrayed again because Oba's story to me was that they hadn't had sex since Ashay was born and they were barely civil to each other. I confronted Oba with all this.

"You know she's crazy. She makes up all these stories. She wants sex with me. She's my son's mother. If she wants it, I have to."

I didn't bother to argue.

In retrospect, I wonder how I ever survived such a snake pit.

In the midst of all this emotional tumult, the publisher offered me a contract to publish my book. I signed the contract and mailed it back. I breathed a prayer of gratitude to Shango and saw one way this would benefit me in the end: I could devote myself to promoting my work, instead of Oba's, without feeling any guilt.

Saturday's Folk Art Market throbbed with glorious color, music and fun. People and artists from all over the world packed the museum plaza. Oba, Ajaka, Shandi and the baby stayed in Ajaka's booth. At one point, I was able to get Shandi's ear and tell her about Oba and Jane. She looked wide-eyed and asked if I knew for sure.

"Yes. I caught him at her house. I talked to her. He confessed. What would I do if I was a woman in Nigeria?"

"In Nigeria, a woman can't do much. It's a man's world. Women must accept it."

"I've had it. I'm not going to help Oba with his business anymore."

"You and Oba have built something together. Don't throw that away."

She quoted a Nigerian proverb, "What you build with your hands, don't destroy with your two feet." She advised me to know where I stand.

"Other women may come and go, but he will always come back to you because you are in business together."

I told Shandi I could almost understand about the other women, but it was the lying I objected to.

"All men lie. All men lie all the time. It's just the way it is."

In the late afternoon, I took the children on a play date. I enjoyed having time with Ashay. We'd developed affection for each other. He felt safe with me. Devmata had hinted that she wanted me to adopt him. Although I'd never wanted children, I entertained the idea.

Tired and hungry, Ashay and I drove through a downpour to Ajaka's house where we were to pick up Oba. Shandi let me in and told me Oba and Ajaka were in the garage. When I walked in the garage, Ajaka walked out talking on the phone. Oba looked down. I asked him how he felt.

"Not good."

He'd lost his cellphone again. They were talking to Jane because she was threatening to throw away all of Oba's things including $8,000 worth of musical instruments and drums.

"She doesn't seem like a vengeful person to me. I'd be surprised if she did that."

"You don't know her."

Ajaka handed the phone to Oba, and he exited into the other room. I told Ajaka that Oba could put his things in my storage if he could get someone to pick them up.

"Marsha, we will all talk about this with Oba, but we must have peace between us."

"If I should get credit for anything, it's for being peaceful under these circumstances. I think I've done amazingly well not to have stabbed Oba with a knife. This doesn't seem to be a big deal with all of you. Is it just the way it is in Nigeria?"

"Don't blame it on Nigeria," Shandi interjected. "It's just the way men are everywhere."

"I can almost buy the 'it's my nature' story, but if you practice polygamy, then put it out in the open. Let everyone involved know what's going on, but if he tells me he's monogamous with me, and he tells her, he's monogamous with her, it's just betrayal and deception."

"Sometimes truth is hard," observed Ajaka.

"And so is this. Lying can cause you to lose all your possessions."

"It's a big topic," said Ajaka. "Let's discuss it later."

Oba returned and gave Ajaka his cellphone back. My cellphone rang.

"Marsha, it's Jane. Are you in a place where you can talk?"

I went into the bedroom and shut the door.

"I've been on the phone with Oba and Ajaka for an hour. Oba has Ajaka telling me that as far as he knows there has never been a romantic relationship between you and Oba, that you are strictly business partners, that you are jealous and just trying to break up me and Oba, that whenever you come to Santa Fe, Oba stays with Ajaka and you stay somewhere else. I don't think you are lying to me, but they almost have me convinced."

"Oba and I have been lovers since before Ashay was conceived. We were together when we met Ajaka. A friend and I invested in a house in Santa Fe. Oba and I sleep there in the same bed."

"Ajaka says Oba is staying with him. Oba is telling me that he hasn't had sex with you in at least a month. When was the last time you had sex with Oba?"

"About two weeks ago. So supposedly we're strictly business partners and have never had a romantic relationship, but he had sex with me a month ago? Hello!"

Jane and I talked for about an hour. She revealed that Oba had been living with her for a year. A YEAR! He slept with her almost every night. I said he hadn't stayed all night with me for about six months, but he certainly had within the last year.

"That would explain some strange stories about all-night gigs."

The instruments Oba and Ajaka were trying to salvage were about $4,000 worth of recording equipment, synthesizers and a keyboard that she bought and gave to Oba as a gift. She had an extra room in her house where she let Oba set up a music studio.

"Jane, if you want Oba, I think he really wants to be with you."

"I'm sure the attraction is mainly financial. I have been very generous with him."

"I wondered where he was suddenly getting money for car insurance and DVD copies."

"All me."

I kept repeating, "A year?" Connecting the dots, I added, "That would mean he was living with you when we went to Puerto Vallarta."

"He went to Puerto Vallarta with you?"

"I paid for Puerto Vallarta. It was our romantic getaway. We stayed with my friends there."

"He told me he was going to New Mexico to work with Ajaka. Ajaka called me and told me about it. Was Ajaka with you?"

"No! It was our romantic vacation!"

"I can't believe this guy. I had gone to Puerto Rico a couple weeks before that. He called me every day while I was there.

Then he went away and didn't call me at all. I was going crazy."

"Yeah, the cellphones don't work from Mexico. I asked him directly at least three times if he was sleeping with you. The first time was after a full moon ceremony, maybe 10 months ago.

"He was already living with me before I ever went to the full moon ceremony."

"I asked him again the day we shot the DVD cover. When he showed up with you, I took him aside and asked him if he'd spent the night with you. He gave me a story about how you were helping him with medications for Ashay, and you left your car somewhere, and he had to take you to get it—and told me not to be so suspicious."

"Of course, he'd spent the night with me. We've been living together for a year."

She told me that after David's accident, Miriam decided she had to stay with David, so Jane went to Big Sur with Oba when he taught the workshop. And on and on. She got him the prescription for antibiotics when he was sick in Santa Fe. She checked him into Cedars-Sinai when the Guillain-Barre was diagnosed. She accompanied him to glaucoma surgery and took care of him afterwards. I was stunned by how the elaborate world of his lies had fooled me.

"His lying makes us not trust our instincts. We feel it. We know. He lies, and we doubt ourselves," I observed.

"And I beat myself up for being a paranoid, suspicious person. Then I hurt myself. I smoke cigarettes. My health has just been terrible in the past year. I have been in so much psychological pain trying to make sense of all the crazy stories he tells me."

"And his health has been going straight downhill."

"Because of the stress, can you imagine how stressful it must be trying to keep all those stories straight? At one point, I said to him 'Oba, when you tell lies, you have to remember who you told what to. If you tell the truth, you don't have to remember anything. It's much easier.'"

She asked me if I lived at Echo Park Avenue and Lucretia.

"Yes. Why?"

"I hate to admit this, but a few months ago, I was so suspicious I hired a private detective and had him followed for days. He was driving all over the city while he was telling me he was at home. One thing I couldn't figure out was why his car was parked for hours at Echo Park and Lucretia."

"Yeah. That's me."

"When does he see you?"

"Since he hasn't been staying all night, it's usually a few hours in the afternoon."

"On Tuesday or Thursday?"

"Yeah, I think so."

"Those are the days I work until 9 p.m."

"And we are the only ones we know about. There could be more."

"I think there are. Do you see him on Sunday between two and four?"

"No."

"I get crazy stories about where he is at that time. I think he's got someone else then."

Jane goes on to tell me her sad history of bad love affairs, the death of her mother, rejection by her father who cheated her out of her inheritance. She started drumming as a way of healing herself from deep depression.

"I can't say that Oba seduced me. I was certainly willing, and there was an immediate, undeniable spark, but he took advantage of me. I told him that he's just a hustler who preys on lonely, vulnerable women."

"That's the insidious thing. He uses his spiritual power to take advantage of women who come to him for healing. It's the same thing as the pedophile priests in the Catholic Church. He doesn't get that it's a violation."

"It's a rape, and I told him I don't like the way he has treated you. I said, 'You've really exploited Marsha badly.'"

Jane wanted to talk to Ajaka again. I took the cellphone into the room, and before I handed it to him, I said to Ajaka in front of the assembled group, "Oba and I are just business partners? As far as you know we've never slept together? He always stays at your house? You are a liar too! How dare you!"

I turned to Oba, "You were living with her when we went to Puerto Vallarta? How dare you!"

Ajaka told Jane that he did not go to Puerto Vallarta. He handed the phone back to me.

Jane asked me to tell Ajaka not to call her tomorrow, to tell Oba his things would be in her storage shed and he could come and get them when he got back to L.A., and to tell Oba not to call her again. She strongly urged me to deal with him the same way.

"He's so sweet and loving. I can't say I've been treated better by any man. You should hear Ajaka on the phone, how smooth he is with the story. They are both hustlers who prey on women. They're both con men and sociopaths. Now I'm going to cry and smoke cigarettes."

I hung up and walked out to the assembled group: Oba, Ajaka, Tookay, Shandi. I was furious, but my voice stayed quiet and calm.

"Get all the drums out of the car now. You are staying here tonight—and come over to the house and get your things."

"Marsha, don't do this," said Shandi, Ajaka and Tookay, almost in unison. Oba sat quiet as a stone. I walked out the door to my car. Oba followed me. I unlocked the car, and he started loading drums into the garage. Thunder cracked like a rifle shot. Shango must have been as angry as I was. The sky opened up and dumped torrents of water on us.

The fiery energy of Shango flared up in me. This *orisha* of anger possessed me. My level-headed composure went up in flames. I threw lightning bolts at Oba and tossed his drums, bags, boxes and everything that belonged to him out on the sidewalk where the pelting rain drenched it. (Moisture ruins goatskin drumheads.) He stood wet and silent. I told him I was going to keep the money we'd made so far to cover the dental bill and travel expenses. He nodded.

When I'd emptied the car, I went back in the house and put my arms around Ashay. Quietly and gently I said, "Ashay, you're going to sleep here tonight. You didn't do anything wrong. I'm just mad at your dad. He and Ajaka will come over to my house and get all your things." Ashay started to cry. I held him close to me and said, "You will be all right. They will take good care of you here."

"See Marsha, you are making that little boy cry."

"Shandi, I don't think it's me."

"Don't do this, Marsha."

"Watch who you stand up for, Shandi. You will have your turn at this."

I walked out.

When Oba came to get his things, I followed him and closed the bedroom door behind us. Shango's fire had purified me. My delusion was burned away.

"I am very sorry that I did this."

"That Ajaka was in this with you shows me how little you both value my work. I feel deeply disrespected. And that you were telling her we never had sex hurts like a knife in my chest."

He nodded.

"This may be the best thing that ever happened to you if you use it as an opportunity to heal yourself."

Silence.

"If you don't, I will write this story. I will expose you."

He became abrupt and all business. Ashay wanted to take the inflatable bed we'd bought. I told him he could. Oba told him to put it back.

"We don't need anything from her."

"Let's not make Ashay suffer because of us."

"Come on, Ashay. Let's go."

I hugged Ashay.

"This is not about you. You've been wonderful and a pleasure to be with. I like you very much."

"Thank you, Marsha," Ashay replied sweetly, and they left.

I cried a little then fell into dreamless sleep. The next day, I called Jane and talked until my cellphone battery went dead. She told me that besides buying Oba his own music studio and setting it up in her house, she was giving him an allowance of $500 a month. She had been upset by being stood up a couple of times early in the relationship, so she asked him to move in with her and promise monogamy. For Oba, $500 a month would be a powerful incentive to lie.

She added that she got Oba to go to a psychotherapist with her to work on some of these issues. Specifically, she wanted to tell me about their relationship, and Oba didn't want her to because, although we weren't sleeping together, I would get mad. The joint psychotherapy session wasn't productive, so she went back herself without Oba. The therapist urged her to call me herself, but she didn't want to go behind Oba's back. The therapist pushed her on it, but she wouldn't do it.

"Now I wish I had called you a long time ago."

Denial is a powerful drug indeed. Oshun possessed me, Jane and Devmata. We were so hungry for the sweetness of love that we agreed to drink Oba's Kool-Aid and ignore the acrid stench of deception. The bitter aftertaste of truth unmasks the vastness of our need. As much as I saw myself as a smart, savvy, spiritual woman, I was an easy mark, just like Jane and Devmata. Estrangement from my family and the despair of my divorce left a gaping open wound just beneath my brave exterior. Oba spotted the vulnerability I hid from the world and played into it.

Besides mourning the death of my love for Oba, I was feeling the loss of belonging to this African village. The revelation that they were stabbing me in the back, while I was celebrating the birth of their child and facilitating her naming ceremony, meant the family I thought I had was just a sham. Ajaka, Shandi, Tookay, Katunga were all players in Oba's emotional con game. Including me in the warmth and camaraderie of clan celebrations was a brilliant ploy to get me to contribute my resources and talents to their community. It was a subtle, sophisticated variation on the Nigerian scam, and I walked right into it.

Much worse was the realization that I'd been spending my energy promoting a business that was completely out of integrity. By representing Oba to the world as a loving healer, I'd been the unwitting pimp for a dangerous predator. I'd been scammed, but I'd also slowly morphed into one of the scammers. Although I was the victim of betrayal and deception, I was also a betrayer and a deceiver. I lost myself and found myself face-to-face with my shadow, and it was not a pretty sight. Like Shango, I needed to hang myself in atonement, at least metaphorically. What could I do to find redemption? How could this crisis transform me?

I woke up at 3 a.m. with my mind churning. I remembered when I said to Oba that maybe his role was simply to play Eshu for me, he said coldly, "You are Eshu too." He was my trickster, and I was his. My threat to reveal his darkness to the world felt like betrayal to him.

Jane called the next day and told me that Oba had agreed to go to therapy with her to try to work things out. I almost choked when she said if he was responsive enough to satisfy her, she would let him move back in.

"I want to find a therapist who will really be tough on him."

"Oba will make a mockery of talking therapy."

"People do change."

"Yes, if they have a lot of motivation and work very hard at it. Oba's an addict—to sex, falling in love and marijuana. He would have to do a 12-step program or lots of sweatlodges and ceremonies to change that."

"I'm going to my therapist tomorrow. He'll probably kick my butt."

"For your sake, I hope so."

Oba called me five days after I threw his drums out of my car into the storm. His voice sounded terrible.

"You want revenge. You want to smear my name and keep me from working."

"I didn't mean it as revenge, but I will tell the truth. I will not keep your secrets, but I will not say anything that's not true."

"I am only a human being. There are stories like this one throughout history, even in the Bible. I didn't murder anyone. I didn't steal from anyone. I just didn't want to hurt anyone."

"Exactly, all the great stories have betrayal in them—Ogun and Oshun, Shango and Oya. It is how the characters heal or don't heal that is what the story is about. This is the part where we bring Eshu out from behind our heads and honor him. Not just you, me too, and Jane. We're all living a great story. The story itself can help heal other people. That's why we are living it."

I reported the receipts I had from the tour so far. He refused to tell me how much he made selling CDs at the Folk Art Market, then he accused me of hiding cash from him.

"I let you handle all the cash on the other tours, and I never complain!"

"We always sit down together and count all the money at the end of the tour. What would you have to complain about?"

"You only care about the money!"

There it was, the same accusation that ended my marriage. After I supported my husband for 18 years, he said, "We wouldn't be having these problems if you weren't so materialistic." After all the help I'd given Oba, all the hours and energy I'd put in, all the times I didn't take my share because he needed the money, all the money I advanced him, all the travel, great sex and beautiful ceremonies, he said, "You only care about the money." It knocked the wind out of me.

"Oba, please be fair so I don't lose money after everything else I've been through on this tour. What do you think is fair?"

"You have the cash."

"OK. That covers expenses to date, not counting the dental bill, and now we need to get home. Will you pay for the gas to L.A.?"

"Why not?"

"Is that a yes?"

"Yes!" He was screaming and out of control.

"Let's work this out later."

I went back and looked at the ledger of money he owed me. He incurred all the expenses after he was living with Jane. It started with the eye drops for his glaucoma. Then he added other medications plus a $100 cash advance, a $400 car repair and the dental bills. I put all that on my credit cards while he was living with a doctor who could have gotten the medications, and who was giving him $500 a month. Was he getting me to pay for things for the sport of it?

Yes, I wanted revenge! Was that so wrong considering the way he'd treated me? I suspected what he really feared was that my warning would scare away his future prey.

Oba called back that evening.

"Ajaka will drive me to Sedona. I'll give you cash when you meet me there."

"I decided I'm not going to Sedona. I don't feel safe with you. You'll have to figure out another way to get home."

"No problem. Devmata will pick me up in Sedona. I'll pay you when I see you in L.A."

"You were really abusive today. I felt like you were out of your mind and capable of killing me and dumping my body in the desert."

He laughed. I suspected Oba's anger could be as murderous as what he related in the story of Ogun.

In his later years, Ogun was a king and a great warrior. He left the

*city and went to fight in a war zone. In a fierce battle, he killed
everyone. On the way home alone, exhausted and bloody from combat,
he saw some people drinking and making merry. He said, "I'm so
thirsty" and asked them for a drink. The people were all very drunk,
and they didn't recognize him because his regal clothes were covered in
blood. He asked them for palm wine. They said, "Sorry, there's no more
palm wine." Ogun thought, "I suffered for these people. I fought for
these people, and they won't give me an ordinary glass of wine?" He
saw many gourds filled with wine. He thought the people were lying to
him. He got so angry, he killed everybody. Then he looked into the
gourds, and they were empty. The people were telling him the truth. He
was remorseful and went back into the jungle where he lived for the rest
of his life. He was too angry to live among people. When you make
sacrifice to Ogun, you take it into the bush where he lives.*

I called Jane and told her I'd decided not to drive Oba back to
L.A. She revealed that Oba told her the recording equipment
didn't matter to him anymore, he just wanted to be with her, then
she added, "But that could be a very high level of manipulation
too." I concurred.

"Oba told me that he fell out of love with you because you
were so demanding."

"Demanding? I never asked him for anything but honesty."

"But you admit you wanted sex with him."

"Yes, but we'd been having great sex for 10 years."

This information, and the way she told it to me, hurt deeply.

Jane wondered if taking Oba to Zen meditation would heal
him. That idea made me laugh. Oba was the greatest Zen master
of all. Her Zen master would simply bow down before him. No
one was more in the moment than Oba. Zen teaches us to accept
that yin and yang must coexist in balance. Oba embodied this
perfectly: liar and lover, priest and predator, sociopath and
shamanic healer. He was all of these things at once. He danced
on that curving edge between the black and white sides of the
circle.

I left Santa Fe reluctantly and drove through bright heat and thundering downpours toward Los Angeles. On the way, I got a phone call from Oba, who was in L.A. He told me he'd moved back into Jane's. After some small talk, I asked him why he called. He said he didn't want me calling Jane and Devmata and talking about him.

"Jane and Devmata are my friends, and I will call them if I want to. You can't tell me who I can call."

"Devmata told me you called, and you are dragging my name through the mud. Call them if you want, but don't mention my name. I don't want you talking about me," he screamed, snapping into a sudden rage.

"Oba we are all supposed to be in a healing process together. We need to talk about what happened as part of the healing. You can't tell us what we can talk about, and we will be talking about you for a long time. You should be talking to us about what happened too. Your game doesn't work anymore."

"So now you know I was having sex with you and Jane and Devmata all at the same time. Now everybody knows."

"Yes. You were having sex with all of us. That's one thing. But you were lying to all of us about the others, and that is something else. We need to heal from all of it."

He hung up, fuming.

In the last couple of years, I'd bought into the illusion of monogamy and occasionally allowed unprotected sex. His confession that he was having sex with Devmata and Jane at the same time, certainly without condoms, made me furious with him and even more furious at myself. I put myself in danger and paid a high price for great sex. Fortunately, medical tests revealed that I dodged the bullet. I never contracted any STDs.

When I delivered Oba's things to Jane's house, she announced that she'd decided to break up with him. Oba was defensive as we went over the accounting together. I protested that I was just trying to break even while he was ahead $800. He didn't think I deserved anything more. I explained that I set up the tour, did all the pre-tour promotion, emailed press releases and produced the DVD. Jane jumped in.

"But the musician provides the real value. What you do isn't that important."

"What if Oba plays and no one knows about it. Is there value without an audience?"

"What if there's an audience, and I don't show up?"

"That's a perfect example of why it makes no sense for me to be in business with you."

Jane undermined the point I was trying to make about the value of my contribution.

"But what you do is easy. You have the email list. You just have to push one button."

"I create the list, maintain the list, add to the list, write the advertising, find the venue, book the show, write the press release, contact the media, handle the publicity. All that takes time."

"But you are on a completely different income level from Oba. He's struggling for survival."

"No, I'm not. I'm struggling too. Since it's so easy, you can start doing it."

"I'm not going to do it, but Oba can."

"Oba, is it fair for you to make money while I make none?"

"Take as much as you want!"

"I'll only take enough to reimburse my expenses, but I want you to think about your lack of generosity to me when I've been so generous with my time and energy helping you."

Jane went into her "survival mode" excuse for him. I countered:

"Oba, you are a powerful *babalawo*. You are trained to deal with threats to survival without fear. That you have slipped into compromising your integrity for fear of lack means that you've forgotten your training. You know exactly what focused spiritual practice is. I have seen you work it. You have taught it to me. I wrote down my intention to get my book published at the Shango ceremony. The energy started to move the next day. I will have the book in a year. If I can manifest, you certainly can."

The next week, Oba called and told me he was living at Jane's, then he handed the phone to her. I asked her if she'd stopped smoking. She says she had. I congratulated her. She explained that they'd decided to give it another try, "with an open and honest relationship."

Oba was still living the archetypal drama of the *orishas*, but he'd recast the roles of the goddesses. Jane had won the part of Oshun, and I was relegated to playing the scorned wife, Oya. The goddess of the wind blew into me. I felt furious about being betrayed and discarded, but I felt strong in my embrace of the truth. I had stepped firmly into Miriam's place, but instead of reacting like she did, with pummeling destruction, I remembered that Oya rules the changes in our lives and owned my power to blow on down the road. As I watched Jane slice off her ear, Oba's Shango looked like a pitiful pretender to the god of fire's throne. I decided to exit laughing and move to the City Different in the Land of Enchantment.

September 2006

Exactly two months after the first confrontation with Jane, all my worldly possessions were on the way to Santa Fe. I watched Los Angeles recede in my rearview mirror. Once I crossed the border into New Mexico, the drive became gorgeous. Rain painted the desert in many shades of green sprinkled with cheerful yellow flowers. When I got to my new home, those bright yellow daisies bloomed everywhere like gold coins scattered in my path.

Chapter 6

Breaking the Spell

I hired Katunga and Kori to unload my furniture. As we worked, Katunga asked me, "What will happen with Oba's music?"

"What do you mean?"

He explained that Oba performed old, traditional songs and rhythms almost completely lost in Nigeria. Katunga said he heard Kilele, one of the songs in Oba's repertoire, sung when he was about two or three, and not since. He said even Ajaka, a ninth generation drummer, had never been taught the rhythms Oba teaches, which meant that they were lost before Ajaka's father's time. Katunga explained that he, Ajaka and all the younger musicians wanted to learn from Oba and record him to preserve as much of his knowledge as possible. Although I'd always instinctively known that what Oba did was important, I hadn't realized that he was the last vestige of an endangered sacred tradition in his own country. I asked Katunga if he thought Oba was a real *babalawo*.

"Yes! You saw the naming ceremony."

"I know Oba can move Spirit, but I'm not Nigerian, and I don't know what the chants mean."

"He's absolutely for real, and you don't see things like that naming ceremony in Nigeria anymore because everyone wants to be modern."

Suddenly, I felt responsible for the loss of an ancient tradition. I hadn't just fallen in love with a man who did me wrong, I also fell in love with the power and beauty of an indigenous religion's music, dance, trance magic and mythology. Breaking off my relationship with Oba could disconnect me from a spiritual life that I treasured, that could easily be lost to the world. I wanted to break up with Oba, but I didn't want to break up with Ifa.

I reached out to try to heal the rift between me and Ajaka. He asked me if I would be willing to help him and his band in the future.

"I don't trust you enough to help you. You lied to me, and you lied about me. Maybe you and Oba think what you did was OK, but I feel like I was treated badly. You have a relationship with me that's separate from your relationship with Oba."

"Oba is living an African life in America. Once you get three or four wives, you have to lie. It seems normal to me."

That comment confirmed what Funmilayo told me: Women don't like polygamy. It may be acceptable to the culture, but only to the men of the culture. Oba and Ajaka's defense seemed to be that they didn't think they were doing anything wrong. I saw the irony that Marsha, queen of diversity and tireless advocate for cross-cultural tolerance, was angry at Nigerian men for acting like Nigerian men. I got that it was a cultural difference, that they saw women (and maybe other people in general), as resources to be exploited.

I wanted to ask: *If it's OK to lie to women to make your life easier, is it OK to lie to people you are in business with? Is it OK to lie to your parents? Is it OK for political leaders to lie? Is it OK to run Internet scams offering millions of dollars to strangers who believe sad stories about dying widows needing to give away a fortune to do God's work?* I get these spam emails almost every day. Can lying, cheating and conning people out of money and resources be dismissed as a cultural difference? Don't we have to draw a line between cultural difference and abuse? Surely, female genital mutilation is a cultural difference as well as torture and a human rights violation. The kidnapping and attempted murder of young women seeking education is a cultural difference and crime. Duplicitous behavior and misrepresentation to secure material and sexual advantage is fraud, pure and simple, no matter how "normal" it is among the men of a culture.

"Ajaka, if you need to lie about something to make it work, it isn't working! I'm telling you that in our relationship, it's not OK for you to lie to me or to lie about me. If you want me to help you with anything, I have to feel like you are loyal to me."

November 2006

At the end of Liz's Saturday African dance class, Katunga announced that Henriette died. The dancers reeled with shock and grief. Many of them knew Henriette. People cried, including me. We joined hands in a circle and offered a prayer. Afterwards, I went over to Ajaka's and got the whole story. Henriette was on her way back to Nigeria after spending the summer performing in Santa Fe. She joined her husband in Brooklyn. Unknown to us, she was eight months pregnant. She went into early labor. Her husband took her to a Brooklyn hospital. She was bleeding badly, so they delivered the baby early but were unable to save her.

Ajaka and Katunga had been up all night talking to her husband and trying to reach relatives in Africa. The confused, grief-stricken husband, who couldn't communicate much information, was estranged from her family. Ajaka was trying to be the go-between. The hospital promised an autopsy would be completed Monday, then the body had to be moved somewhere. The baby was in intensive care and would be hospitalized for several weeks. Henriette's family wanted the body sent home, which would cost $15,000. Of course, no one had that kind of money, but cremation was vetoed because of cultural taboos.

I stayed all afternoon trying to help, offering suggestions and being supportive. I called Jane. Since she was a doctor, I thought maybe she would be able to call the hospital and get more information. She felt the hospital would be reluctant to tell her anything because of malpractice fears and because the information was confidential. She called back later and said she talked to a friend who had a body shipped from L.A. to Africa for $7,000.

Henriette left ten children without a mother—four of hers and six by her husband and his previous wife. Her baby, Buki, died of a tropical disease about a year before. My heart went out to all the women in the world who face this danger every day with such great courage. My heart went out to the baby who just entered this world through sudden tragedy. Henriette was 29, a vibrant high-energy spirit and loving mother.

That night, I cried myself to sleep. It was just so sad.

When we reconvened at Ajaka's on Monday, Kori joined the group. He'd also been in contact with Henriette's husband and reported that the husband was so grief-stricken and hysterical he didn't want to see the baby. We tracked down the airline that would ship the body for $7,000. I advocated for a local burial or cremation so that huge chunk of money could go toward taking care of the children, but the family wouldn't consider it. They were adamant that she had to be buried in the soil of her village. The Nigerians were willing to spend significant resources to get Henriette's dead body back, but they seemed to have no interest in nurturing her child, the living legacy of their departed beloved. This was a cultural difference that I found dark and difficult to understand.

We brainstormed about how to raise the funds. The Nigerians committed to contributing $300 each. Another musician friend and I contributed $200 each. That was around $1,500. I suggested asking Liz's dance class for donations. The class drew 50 to 80 dancers three times a week. All were devoted to African music and dance.

The next Saturday after class, Ajaka made an appeal, and we passed a hat. The contributions were generous and continued to come in throughout the week. Eventually, the total came to almost $3,500. Henriette's family in Nigeria managed to scrape together the last $2,000. The baby survived and became healthy enough to leave the hospital but not healthy enough to travel to Nigeria. Accompanying his wife's body home was the father's highest priority, so a foster family in Brooklyn took the baby. The idea of the baby being cared for by strangers disturbed Kori. He felt strongly that her American family was in Santa Fe. The other Nigerians quietly agreed. Kori insisted that we must find someone to take care of her. Ajaka and Shandi said they couldn't handle it because they had their own baby. Katunga and his girlfriend also bowed out. Kori's wife didn't have time to care for an infant because she was in law school. I thought it was a long shot, but I suggested that Kori inquire at dance class.

When he did, to my amazement, an elder white woman, Shirley, raised her hand.

"I'll do it. I've just retired. I have time, and she needs to be loved."

Again the hat was passed, and Kori collected enough money to fly the foster mother and child to Santa Fe. A week later, the foster mother delivered the baby to Shirley during dance class. She hadn't been named yet, so we decided to call her Buki Two temporarily. Shirley brought her to dance class every week so she could listen to the drumming from her carrier. Nursing mothers in the class volunteered to nurse her. Other women signed up for babysitting shifts to relieve Shirley.

After a year and a half of loving care, the baby's father decided he was ready to take her to Nigeria and care for her himself. He arrived and Shirley quietly handed her over and wished them well. I saw the nurturing love of Yemoja embodied in Shirley. I felt proud to be a member of a dancing village that mothered an abandoned child. The true spirit of Ifa lives in these loving women.

December 2006

Oba went to Africa for a month, at Jane's expense, even though she didn't join him because she couldn't get off work. The night after Christmas, as my elderly black cat slept beside me in my bed in Santa Fe, I dreamed about Oba opening a new Yoruba spiritual center. In the dream, I went there with Devmata.

Women crowded the center, and he put his hands on a beautiful African-American in a golden headwrap to bless her. I said to Devmata, "We can be sure he's sleeping with her." As I looked around the center, I realized all the women were his lovers. He walked away to avoid me, and I followed him into a backstage area. While I was watching he transformed into an old hag of a witch, naked with sagging skin, covered with sores, wearing an elaborate ancestor mask. He/she started dancing and moved toward me menacingly. I felt afraid… then my cat's fierce growls woke me up. In waking reality, the cat was hissing at some invisible being in the room. Had the cat been dreaming the dream with me? Could he see my dream? Was there real danger in my bedroom?

Oba was in Africa. He could have been sending dark energy to me, maybe with the help of other sorcerers, but I wasn't afraid. I knew it wouldn't work because Oba had taught me that a curse won't stick to the innocent. I was innocent and a well-trained warrior. Although the dream and my cat's reaction unnerved me, I knew I was safe.

2007

On New Year's Day, the morning sweatlodge I'd planned to attend got canceled because the firewood was under three feet of snow. Instead, I was invited to an impromptu pipe ceremony with an Oneida medicine man who practiced bear medicine. After he sang and rattled, he went into a trance, laid his hands on each participant and growled. The bear worked on me for a long time. He blew smoke and pushed on my heart area as he growled. He told me that someone put something in me to drain my life force, and I needed sweatlodge healing as soon as possible to get rid of it. I knew Oba had done it in the dreamtime, and I knew I had all the tools I needed to heal it.

After the ceremony, a Native medicine woman who was present told me that she saw a little green man in my chest who entered through my back and got caught in my heart area. She described him as shiny and metallic like a Christmas ornament. She also saw darts like porcupine quills in my back that had been thrown at me by jealous people. I told her about Oba and the dream.

"West African? That's why I've never seen it before. I bet he's throwing up right now."

Metallic green is the color of Ogun. Did Oba send the *orisha* of war to kill me? Ogun embodies life force, the warrior, the one who cuts through obstacles. A little Ogun inside of me didn't have to be malevolent, but the darts in my back needed to be removed and a shield of protection created. Since the dream, I'd noticed a pricking sensation at a particular place near the base of my neck.

When I got home, I went to my altar, lit my candles and prayed to Spirit to guide me to heal myself. I spoke to the little green man.

"Ogun, thank you for visiting me. I honor your power. While you are here, could you help me remove these darts from my back? Please pull them out and take them back to Oba in Africa."

He appeared in my mind and nodded that he would help. He roamed around my back and pulled out several darts. He was loving and gentle. A dart at the base of my neck stuck stubbornly, and he had to work it out. When he was finished, he held a whole armload of darts. I thanked him.

"When you see Oba in Africa, thank him for sending you. Tell him that I'm sending these gifts back to him with love because I didn't ask for them and I don't need them. Tell him that he doesn't need to be afraid of me."

Then I pushed Ogun away from me with a wave of energy. He waved to me as he flew off to Africa.

Fortunately, the excitement of my life didn't allow me to spend time focusing on darkness. My book was being published in early August. It was printed! Boxes of books arrived at the house. It looked beautiful! I was proud. I planned a launch party and scheduled promotional events.

July 8, 2008

I was in the pharmacy picking up eye drops prescribed for the cataract surgery I'd had the day before. I was marveling at my sudden clear vision, both literal and metaphoric, when my cellphone rang. It was Charles, Oba's drumming student in Sedona. I heard a jumble of words that included "Oba," "accident," "killed" and "coma." I couldn't comprehend what he was saying and asked him to repeat it.

"Oba was in a terrible accident last night on his way to Sedona. He's in a coma in a hospital in Flagstaff. Ashay was killed."

I froze.

"I thought you'd want to know."

"My God!"

Charles explained that Oba scheduled a workshop in Sedona on the way to Santa Fe for the Folk Art Market. Charles talked to him about 9 p.m., and Oba said he was on the road and would arrive that night. When he didn't show up or answer his cellphone, Charles called Jane. When she couldn't get an answer, she did a 911 search on Oba's cellphone and located him in the hospital in Flagstaff. Charles said Jane would drive to Flagstaff. I thanked him for letting me know and asked him to keep in touch with any news.

While I was talking to Charles, Ajaka called on the other line. I called him back. He'd just gotten a call with the same news. Neither of us knew what to say or do. Ajaka asked, "Should we go there?"

"I don't know. Let's think about it and talk in a while."

I wasn't processing information very well. I went home, put away the groceries, and cried.

A million things went through my head: *It was bound to happen.*

He was always falling asleep at the wheel, leaving hours late, tired, stoned and sleep-deprived. I was the one who would keep him awake or insist we stop at a motel. Poor Ashay! Why did he have to die? If I hadn't broken up with Oba, I would have been in the car. I could have been killed, or I would have kept him awake or made him rest. Maybe I didn't protect Ashay enough. If Oba lives, he will never forgive himself—and maybe, rightfully so. If he lives, he may go to prison for child endangerment and vehicular manslaughter. Surely there was marijuana in the car and in his blood. I'm grateful that I got out of that situation in time to save my own life. Clear vision? Now I see that Oba is, and always was, on a path to destruction. I saved myself just in time.

I called Edna, a friend and longtime student of Oba's in Albuquerque who was expecting Oba to stay with her. She thought we should leave immediately and fly there. I didn't think I should go, because all his other women were sure to show up, and my presence would just make everyone more upset. Edna thought she should go because she was a nurse and not one of his lovers.

Ajaka called and said according to the Highway Patrol, it happened at three a.m. No other cars were involved. Oba hit the rail at full speed, and the car flipped. Ashay was killed instantly, his skull crushed by the roof of the car.

"Maybe Oba needs you there."

One of Oba's drumming students from L.A. called me to be sure I knew. He said that Oba was conscious when they checked him in. The steering wheel hit him hard. He had a broken arm that would need surgery and bruised lungs. He was having trouble breathing, so they put him on a respirator and sedated him. He didn't think he was in a coma. He asked me if I would go.

"I think it would just make all the other women mad."

"Maybe not. Miriam, Devmata and Jane are all going together."

"They are? They put down their weapons?"

"Yes. They are coming together for this."

Then I wanted to go. If all the women were coming together at the hospital, I should be there too. It would either be a mutual healing or the ultimate catfight.

Ajaka was worried he wouldn't get back in time for the Folk Art Market opening performance. I called Edna. She agreed to drive with me.

When Edna and I arrived in Flagstaff, we ran into Jane, Miriam, Devmata and Charles in the hospital hallway. The women seemed comfortable with each other. They all flew from L.A. together. Jane paid for the tickets. I hugged each one and told Devmata how sorry I was about Ashay. She smiled a sad smile and expressed concern for Oba. Miriam put her arm around Devmata.

"This poor mother is going to need help with expenses. I hope you can help with that."

Edna and I went to Oba's room while the others went on a mission to recover Oba's personal effects. He was unconscious with the respirator tube taped into his mouth, hooked up to a bank of monitors, tubes running in and out of him everywhere. His upper lip was swollen and split. Bandages swaddled his left arm. I whispered to him. His eyes blinked a couple times, and he moved a hand violently like he wanted to pull the tubes out, but restraints limited it. We sat in his room in silence for a long time. I contemplated this man whom I had loved to the point of obsession. His sparkling charisma, spiritual power and sexual potency had left him. My aching desire for him left me. He was just a broken body, powerless and inert. And worse, this man I'd idolized as a spiritual leader was responsible for the death of his own son. I truly tasted the bitter. The death of an innocent child was not part of the archetypal mythology that ruled our lives. Oshun's spell was broken.

When the women got back, a doctor told us that Oba had no

broken bones, no spinal cord injury and no apparent brain damage. He was a lucky man. Jane sat right beside him and held his hand. Miriam hovered nearby. Devmata sat at his feet. Edna and I retreated to a sofa in the corner. No one knew if Oba knew that Ashay was dead. The nurses told us that they were going to lower his sedative dose and try weaning him off the respirator the next day.

Edna and Jane agreed that it was "just an accident that could have happened to anybody." I objected, saying Oba made an irresponsible choice by leaving so late and not getting a motel when he got sleepy. He needed to face that and take responsibility for it so he could change his behavior. Both women accused me of placing blame and not being compassionate. I pointed out that there is a difference between blame and responsibility—and that guilt would be an appropriate emotion for Oba to feel when he found out that he killed his son.

In the morning, we got to the hospital just as Miriam arrived. As we walked into the building, Miriam complained about how Jane monopolized Oba and enabled his irresponsible behavior. Miriam told us how Al-Anon saved her by making her realize that she had to separate from Oba for her own good and the good of her son. In the elevator, Miriam lectured us about only bringing positive energy into the room, insisting we must leave any anger or negativity outside in Oba's best interest. Edna and I agreed with her. She turned to me and said, "I can tell you are angry, Marsha. You have to leave that outside."

When we got into the room, we found Oba sitting up breathing on his own with Jane holding his hand. He seemed filled with wonder that all these women were together. I hung back, but he saw me and gave me a smile so warm and glowing that it surprised and unnerved me.

Jane asked us to step outside with her. In the waiting room, she told us that as soon as Oba was breathing on his own and the tube was removed, two policemen appeared and ordered her out of the room. They told Oba about Ashay with no one else present. Jane's voice got shaky and emotional at the thought of Oba hearing this news without her there to protect him. She said he was upset and agitated when she was allowed back in the room. Clearly, she was agitated too.

Miriam went to call Devmata while Jane, Edna and I returned to Oba's room. Jane rushed to his side. In Jane's eyes, Oba was a lost boy, a bewildered stranger in a strange land, now literally helpless. Being the most competent caretaker, the one with healing knowledge and financial resources, made her the special one.

We did not talk about Ashay. Oba, still hooked up to monitors, a chest tube, catheter, oxygen, seemed slightly confused and disoriented. As a nurse changed the dressing on Oba's arm, Jane told her she wasn't doing it right. The nurse ignored her.

Miriam came back in the room and immediately tried to wedge herself between Oba and Jane. In Miriam's eyes, Oba was her husband, the partner who stuck with her through conflicts and infidelities. His talent and charisma gave her legitimacy. Her management gave her power over him. Being the one legal and legitimate wife made her the special one. Miriam turned on Jane and attacked.

"You are so disrespectful of me and our family," indicating herself and Oba. "You never consider that anyone else may need time with Oba. I'm the only one who has the legal right to make decisions for Oba. I should be next to him all the time."

"But I'm the one who lives with him. I know what he wants better than you. I'm a doctor, and I know his whole medical history. I'm the best qualified to make decisions about his well-being, besides he's conscious now. He can make decisions for himself."

"Get away from my husband. You have no right to be here. Now you will be forced to respect my marriage."

I offered a soft, "Miriam, you might want to dial back that

anger." She ignored me and wiggled beside Oba pushing Jane out of the way. Oba looked stunned and confused and said nothing.

Devmata, who'd been making funeral arrangements, showed up just as Jane was about to explode. In Devmata's eyes, Oba was her passionate lover, the one who kept returning to her bed, the one who gave her his child, the child who was now lost forever. Being forgiving and long-suffering made her the special one.

"There she is. The mother of that poor boy is here," purred Miriam. "Please give the two of us some time alone with Oba for healing."

That poor boy? Miriam hated him from the moment he was born. She never allowed him in her house. She threatened and abused Devmata and did everything she could to keep the boy's father away from him. Devmata docilely let Miriam sit her in a bedside chair.

As soon as Oba regained consciousness, these women returned to competing like rival Nigerian wives. Each one of them believed Oba's lie that they were special. I realized that telling a woman she's special was the easiest lie for a man because we are so ready to believe it, and it excuses his abuse, deceptions and lack of integrity. Just like all of them, I was ready to believe that lie. I felt special as the competent caretaker, the powerful manager, the one true partner, the passionate but long-suffering lover. I was one of them. I was exactly like all the women who spin a story to make themselves believe they are special. That epiphany burned away the remnants of my illusions. Oba's power over me went up in smoke.

Edna and I walked the steaming Jane out of the room and sat with her in the waiting room. We tried to talk Jane down as she went into victimhood.

"Why do I have to wear the scarlet letter, just because I love him and take care of him?"

I tried to explain that Miriam always pulled this shit.

Devmata and I had both worn the scarlet letter for years. Jane was just beginning to see Miriam's nasty manipulative ways, but we were not surprised. Jane wept.

"But how can she act like this if she has Oba's best interests at heart? It's like she's cutting the baby in two."

I explained that Miriam had never had Oba's best interests at heart. As long as I'd known her, she'd only cared about her power over him.

"The darkest, most cynical part of me thinks Miriam is being so supportive and loving towards Devmata because she's secretly delighted that Ashay is dead," I added. "Now the evidence of Oba's infidelity is erased forever."

Jane admitted that she thought the same thing.

"Miriam sees this as her chance to regain the throne as queen to Oba's king. She will do whatever it takes to make that happen," I continued.

Jane worried that Miriam was berating Oba and asked Edna to go look in the room. Edna came back with a report that they were all holding hands and singing. Jane flew into a fury about being left out.

Finally, Miriam and Devmata appeared in the waiting room. Jane and Miriam attacked each other—with Miriam taking the lead. Devmata stepped into the hall to make a phone call. Miriam berated Jane for trying to steal her family, the only one she ever had since her own parents were so critical and unloving. Her family disowned her when she married Oba, yet his family came from Africa with gifts for her. She felt they were the family she always wanted, even though she had to leave Oba to save herself and her son.

Miriam turned on me and told me how hard she worked to make Ifa Center happen, only to have friends like me betray her and break up her family. She told Jane and me that Oba was only interested in us for our money. She lamented that she was deeply hurt when I paid for his hernia surgery, and when she went to the hospital to be with him, they wouldn't let her go up to the room because I was there. She was forced to go home alone where she cried all day. I listened quietly then offered that I'd never had any money.

"I took Oba through the county welfare system to get that surgery. When he was in recovery, a nurse came in and said his wife was on the phone asking if she could come to the room, and Oba said 'Yes.' But you never showed up. You just called and talked to him on the phone."

Miriam ignored my story.

Then Jane started her story of dysfunctional family life: Her parents were Communist lawyers and atheists. After her mother died, her father, whom she thought was Mr. Monogamous, remarried immediately to a woman he'd apparently been having an affair with. Jane hated her stepmother and was ultimately disowned by them. She put herself through nursing school, then medical school and became a doctor, but she'd never had a loving family, never been married, no children. She didn't under-stand why they couldn't all just get along and be one big happy family. Miriam scoffed and seethed at that idea.

I went to check on Devmata and found her wandering the hall. She wanted to see Ashay's body, but the coroner wouldn't allow it until the body was in a funeral home. She wanted to get a copy of the police report and the autopsy. I promised to help her. Devmata confessed that she had to leave the room because she couldn't stand to see Miriam telling lies and blaming everybody else, "just like the old days."

Back in the waiting room, Jane was spinning out about how Miriam had been turning the nurses against her so she wouldn't be allowed in, how Miriam let her pay for everything then conspired against her. Miriam gloated. She'd succeeded in making Jane look like the crazy one.

When I had a moment alone with Oba, he whispered to me.

"I messed up big this time."

"Yes, you did. Don't let Ashay die for nothing. Stop doing things that hurt people who love you. All you have to do is live the teachings of your religion."

"We'll see. God is the supervisor."

"Yes, God is the supervisor, and Oba is the carpenter. The supervisor is telling the carpenter to get busy on that remodeling job."

Back at our hotel, I commented to Edna about the similarities between Jane and Miriam's stories. Both came from dysfunctional families, disowned by parents, finding the family they never had in Oba's harem. In fact, I had a similar story—not wanted by my parents, disowned when I married a man of a different race, put myself through school without their support. Although I didn't think I was looking for family, Oba hooked into my unconscious need.

By the time I met Devmata in the morning, Jane had a whole drama to tell. When she went to the hospital at 5 a.m., the nurses called security. Two guards came to the room brandishing handcuffs and dragged her out, forbidding her to ever come back into the hospital. She was convinced that Miriam poisoned all the nurses against her. The staff questioned whether she was a real doctor. She was so flustered she couldn't remember her medical license number and had to look it up. When she went to a desk to write it down, she was accused of rifling through a doctor's charts, which she said she didn't do. She had claustrophobia and the sight of handcuffs made her panicky. She kept saying she was arrested, which wasn't true. She was just escorted out.

Later we heard the hospital's side of the story: she was wandering around the floor, trying to minister to other patients, reading their charts, giving orders about Oba's care. The staff felt her emotional involvement interfered with their work.

I put Devmata in my car and drove south. When we saw no signs of an accident, I called Highway Patrol, and an officer told me the exact mile markers. He told me that Oba hit the guard rail but ended up in the median, which meant he rolled across all the lanes. Devmata picked wild sunflowers to leave at the site of the crash. At the mile markers, I pulled onto the median with hazard lights flashing. Devmata chanted a Sanskrit mantra as I threw a dozen sunflowers out the window one by one.

Devmata wanted to find out if she could have an open-casket viewing before cremation, so I called the medical examiner. A woman answered who said she wasn't the coroner but was familiar with the case. I put her on the phone with Devmata and prayed that the details of the body's condition wouldn't be gruesome. The woman was helpful and compassionate.

"I have a photo of him on my computer. I'll pull it up, and you can ask me questions." Devmata relayed information to me.

"His face looks pretty good. He could have an open casket if he wears a cap or hat to cover the compound fractures on the top of his skull. The rest of his body isn't terribly disfigured."

Her sweet voice saying such sad words broke my heart open, and I wept.

On the drive back through Oak Creek Canyon, Devmata was calm and philosophical. At the hospital, Oba had been moved out of ICU into a regular room. As we walked in the door, I saw Oba sitting up flanked by two security guards. He looked agitated. My heart jumped into my throat. Were they there to slap the cuffs on him and drag him off for vehicular manslaughter and child endangerment? Did they find marijuana in the car? Two friends from Sedona were in the room, and they looked calm. I tried to sound casual as I spoke to the security guards.

"Hi. What's going on?"

"We're just speaking to this gentleman."

"Oh, does he need security?"

"He asked us to come over and help him with something."

Clearly, they wanted privacy with Oba. We stepped out into the hall.

The friends explained that Oba asked for security so he could complain about Jane being banned from the hospital and try to get her visiting privileges reinstated. When the security guards left, and we went back into the room, Oba was still angry about how Jane was being treated. He worried that she'd leave and go back to L.A. That possibility made him panicky.

I went out in the hall to call Jane. She was spinning out, furious that Oba hadn't defended her, thrown Miriam out, and demanded that the hospital let her back in. She told the story of the handcuffs and being "arrested" again. She was irrational and insisted that Oba must not love her or he would have called security on her behalf sooner.

"Jane, listen to me. Oba is very sick. He did what you wanted him to as soon as he was able. Now he needs you to tell him that you are not leaving so he can get some rest."

"Did he tell them that I didn't do it? I was just writing down my license number. Did you tell him that Miriam poisoned all the nurses' minds against me?"

"Jane, no one has to tell Oba that. He knows Miriam well. She's been doing stuff like that for as long as they've been together. Right now, what Oba needs is your calm voice telling him that you are here for him and you are not going back to L.A. Can you calm down and do that now?"

At last she heard me, "Yes."

I took the phone, went back in Oba's room and found him sitting on the edge of the bed with Devmata kneeling in front of him holding a urine bottle as he moaned in pain while he peed into it. I asked Jane to hold. When he completed his release, I handed him the phone and walked away.

I took Devmata back to the residence. As we walked in, Jane flipped out. I'd predicted that Oba's lawyer would take Miriam's side. He did, mocking Jane with "whatever makes you think you have any rights here when he has a legal wife?"

"They'll be sorry. I'll get my own attorney and sue them all!"

A precious child was dead. Her beloved was badly injured, and Jane was seething because none of us had taken her out to lunch.

"Jane, Devmata and I were in Sedona at the accident scene."

"I'm sorry," Edna apologized, "I took the car to the hospital and was so busy all day helping Oba that I spaced on you being stuck without a car."

Jane started the handcuffs story again.

"You know what they did to me? They came in with handcuffs…"

I flipped.

"Jane, Stop it! Stop telling that story. Ashay's dead. This isn't about you."

"But I'm claustrophobic."

"So what? You got scared. We get it."

"I don't appreciate you telling me to stop feeling what I'm feeling. It doesn't help!"

"I'm not telling you not to feel it. I'm telling you to take it to the Zendo."

"I don't want a philosophy class. I want to express my feelings!"

Edna, ever the mediator, jumped in, "She just wants to be heard."

"I heard you the first three times you told the handcuffs story. Please stop telling it!"

I apologized, but I'd had it with "the matrix" as Edna called the tangle of women.

As we drove back to Albuquerque, Edna told me that according to Jane, before she ever went to bed with Oba, he said that he hadn't had sex for a long time and felt very vulnerable about making love to a woman again. This was while he was getting all the sex he wanted from me and Devmata. We'd all been conned by an absolute master.

October 2008

Edna invited me to an Afro-Cuban dance workshop she'd organized in Albuquerque. The instructor, Padrino, originally from Havana, was a Santeria priest as well as a professional dancer. Although he spoke Spanish, he was totally African with long locks and blue-black skin. Padrino explained that Santeria was the same practice as Yoruba Ifa, simply transplanted to Cuba and translated into Spanish. He reminded me of Oba, but with an even more muscular body that was pretty amazing for a man of 60. When he chanted in Yoruba, he sounded like Oba. In his class, he taught us dances to honor Oya, Ogun, Oshun, Yemoja and Elegba.

After class, he complimented me on my dancing. I told him I spent years with a Yoruba *babalawo* as a student and his lover.

"But no more! *Muchas mujeres!*"

"*Muchas mujeres? Un babalawo?*"

Edna's husband Carlos translated:

"A Yoruba man can have many wives but not a *babalawo*. A *babalawo* must have just one wife. If he has more than one, he may lose things."

Padrino explained that a *babalawo*'s initiation included being buried from the waist down to remind him that his work was entirely spiritual. The woman who helped a *babalawo* made him great. Therefore each *babalawo* had to ask his head *orisha* for permission before he brought any woman into his life. The *babalawo* was supposed to have only one wife because he had only one true helper. If she got mad about other women and left him, all of his helping *orishas* would go with her, and he would lose everything.

Oba certainly did lose everything—twice. Both times were when I left him. The first time Ifa Center burned down. The second time Ashay was killed and Oba's injuries to his arms and lungs prevented him from drumming and singing. In between was David's accident. At that point, I was still with him, but he was secretly living with Jane. Oba was cheating on his own religion all along.

According to Padrino, if a *babalawo* disrespected his one true helper and she left, all the good energy went with her. He kept saying something in Spanish about me having the chicken, the egg and the gold. I couldn't figure it out. Carlos finally explained that it was an idiom meaning I got all the good stuff.

Padrino told me that he saw me thriving and moving into wealth and that many helping *orishas* were with me. He commented that my hair (now naturally pure white) was a crown that deserved respect, and any *babalawo* would know that. He congratulated me on having the strength of character to move on with my life and not settle for the crumbs from Oba's table. He said he could see that I was respectful and a great help to Oba, and he never helped me at all.

If Oba's helping *orishas* were with me, it would explain his obvious joy at seeing me appear unexpectedly in his hospital room. It had nothing to do with me. He was just happy to see his *orishas* coming back to help him. Padrino suggested that I make an altar to Oshun in my home. Of course, that made complete sense. My hurt was blocking my Oshun energy.

During the class, Padrino talked about the complexity of Oshun. She was the only Oludumare trusted to go into the forest and find Ogun to persuade him to use his warrior energy to help humanity instead of destroy it. Of course, she did this by seducing him. Sometimes she appears wearing handcuffs, representing how love can imprison, or how we imprison ourselves when we are in love. In the dance, she breaks the handcuffs off.

July 2009

Oba returned to Santa Fe to play with Ajaka at the Folk Art Market. He was not the same man who was my lover. His body was broken, as was his spirit. Instead of being seduced by sexual charisma, I felt like I was visiting my grandfather. He was still charming, but I could tell by the way he held his body that he was in constant pain. Heavy doses of painkillers made him drowsy and unsteady on his feet. His once-twinkling eyes looked glazed and dull. In place of the fire that had been the light of my life, I saw stone-cold ashes. The handcuffs of love slipped easily off my wrists.

I'd tasted the bitter and the sweet, the salty and the spice. In the mirror of Oba's deceptions, I saw my own flaws. Raw, jagged scars revealed how my own self-deception had damaged my integrity, my self-worth, my heart. My metaphorical ear was only one of the parts of myself that I lost. And yet I gained knowledge of a rich ancient culture. I felt the joy of drum and dance. I dove deep into trance. I embraced the healing energy of the *orishas*. I enjoyed divine, transcendent sex. Although Oba misused Ifa, as followers can misuse any religion, it didn't compromise the power of the dance or the beauty of the ceremonies for me. I still see the joy and truth, the dark and light of life in Ifa.

Epilogue

I dressed in white, took honey and yellow rose petals and went to a deserted spot on the bank of the Rio Grande River. As I waded into the icy water, I prayed to Oshun.

"*Orisha* of love, these offerings are for you. Please take my bitterness. I give you this honey to make you sweet again."

With reverence, I poured the honey in the river. The cold water stiffened the amber liquid, and it stuck to the jar. I scraped it out with my fingers.

"I give you these rose petals in gratitude for the many experiences of love I have lived."

I tossed the petals into the flowing fresh water. I sat on the bank and spoke to Oba.

"I was angry that you deceived me, when of course, I was deceiving myself all along. Now I know you never loved me."

The river answered.

"My Shango loves your Oshun."

"More bullshit..."

Then Oshun herself whispered in my ear.

"No. Marsha, you confused the archetypal love in the stories of the *orishas* with personal love. The Oshun in you and the Shango in Oba embodied and lived the mythic story. But Oba, the man, is wounded and incapable of returning the love you gave him. Personal love must flow both ways to be authentic. Your mistake was holding your love for him precious when he didn't value it. Love can be a virtue or a flaw, depending on whether the object of your love reciprocates. Now you've let go of your personal love for him, but Oshun still lives in you."

"But our sex was powerful and sacred. Is that possible without love?"

"Sex is a force of Nature. It can give you the same sense of oneness with Source as you get when you see a glorious sunset or feel the power of a waterfall. The sunset and the waterfall don't necessarily love you personally, although you are a perfectly lovable woman."

"Loving Oba made me blind. I was insane to stay in such a corrupt situation so long."

"You went through a dark passage of willful self-deception. The Eshu in Oba showed you your shadow, but you found your way through delusion, and the Eshu in you called him on his game. You chose the adventure knowing full well that it was unlikely to end with 'happily ever after.' You were brave enough to explore unknown territory."

"But I feel like something in me is broken."

"Just your heart. It's healing."

"So have I ever known authentic personal love?"

"No, but on this journey, you learned what it is not. Let the river of love carry you. Somewhere in the flow you may find real love, but whether or not you're blessed with it in this lifetime, enjoy riding my rapids."

"Is it more natural to be monogamous or to have multiple partners?"

"The point of the *orisha* myths and the I Wo San is that opposite truths can exist simultaneously, within each person and in our lives. Our dance is to hold them in balance, not to choose one or the other."

I noticed that my rose petals were washing up on a little beach. I gathered them up. Now that they were wet, they were heavier. I thanked Oba for all the good times as I pitched them into the swift current. As I washed my hands and face in the river and said, "Thank you, Oshun, for taking away my hurt and bitterness," I imagined the rose petals traveling past Albuquerque and into the Gulf of Mexico as my restless, broken-open heart rode the river with them.

Endnotes

1, 2, 3, 4, 5, 6, 7, 8, 9, 10, 11

Recordings of these songs and rhythms are featured on the *Honey in the River Soundtrack*, available for download from iTunes, Amazon Music and CD Baby.

References

Books:

The Way of the Orisa, Philip John Neimark, HarperSanFrancisco, 1993

Awo: Ifa and the Theology of Orisha Divination, Awo Fa'Lokun Fatunmbi, Original Publications, Bronx, New York, 1992

Sex at Dawn: How We Mate, Why We Stray and What It Means for Modern Relationships, Christopher Ryan and Cacilda Jetha, Harper Collins, 2010

A History of the Yoruba People, Stephen Adebanji Akintoye, Dakar, 2010

Website:

Lugo Lake Mosuo Cultural Development Association (2006) Walking marriages [online]. Available from: http://www. mosuo-project.org/walking.htm (Accessed November 22, 2014)

Music:

Babatunde Olatunji http://www.olatunjimusic.com

Honey in the River Soundtrack, available on itunes, Amazon Music and CD Baby.

Honey in the River Glossary

Ajaja – Processional song in Ifa ceremony, lyrics translate as "Are there any spirits here?"

Asha – Word for culture or character in the Yoruba language.

Awo – Yoruba word for the esoteric understanding of the invisible forces in Nature which remain awesome and elusive and can only be grasped through direct participation. There's no precise English equivalent, but it refers to the hidden principles that explain the mystery of creation and evolution.

Babalawo – Ifa traditional healer and ceremonial leader.

Bata – Drum associated with the cult of Shango, also called Thunder Drum. It can be three small attached cylinders played with stiff leather sticks or a double-headed cylinder played with hands.

Candomble – Indigenous Afro-Brazilian religion based on Ifa.

Diaspora – A group of people who live outside the lands where their ancestors lived, or the place where those people currently live, such as African communities outside of Africa.

Djembe – African drum with a goat-skin head on a chalice-shaped wooden shell, played with hands.

Djun djun – Double-headed cylindrical drum played with sticks. *Djun djun* drives the tempo in African drum ensembles.

Ebo – Offerings made to the *orishas*.

Egungun – A masked dancer who channels the wisdom of ancestors. While in trance, the dancer may deliver messages from the ancestors to the celebrants.

Elegba – Community shadow. See Eshu.

Eshu – Trickster *orisha* who lives behind our head and pushes us to make mistakes. He whispers in our ear to get us to make bad choices. When he is acknowledged, he will come out in front of our face where we can see him and honor him. Then he becomes the messenger to all the other *orishas*. He's always honored first in every ceremony. He colors are red and black. He has goat horns and hooves. He is our shadow. Eshu makes his home at the crossroads. His companion is the vulture. He likes cigars, wine, whisky, chili and African alligator pepper. He uses the shepherd's crooked stick to keep us in line.

Go do – Mid-range notes of the *djembe* played with the fingers only as the knuckles at the top of the palm rest on the rim.

Gun – Bass note of the *djembe* played with an open palm in the center of the drumhead.

Huichol – Indigenous people in west central Mexico known for using peyote in religious ceremonies and creating bright, psychedelic bead work and yarn paintings. They call themselves Wixarika.

I Ching – Chinese divination system in which patterns of tossed coins or yarrow sticks refer to classic oracular texts in a *Book of Changes*.

Ifa – Indigenous religion of the Yoruba people from Nigeria, West Africa.

Ile Bobo, Ile Orisha – Song invoking *orisha* Obatala, used to call in the four directions in Ifa ceremony.

Ile Re Ogun – Song invoking *orisha* Ogun, usually the final song of Yoruba ceremony.

Iyoya – Song associated with *orisha* Yemoja, in the Bendel language from mid-western Nigeria.

Kilele – Song asking, "What's going on?"

Obatala – *Orisha* of creation and creativity. He made the land, then he made the people out of clay. He's represented as a white-bearded old man with a walking stick. His color is pure white. His offerings are white flowers and white candles.

Ochosi – *Orisha* of the hunt, intuition and shamanic power. He's an archer who lives in the forest who doesn't have to aim to hit the target. His symbol is the bow and arrow. Ogun is his brother.

Odu – A book of Ifa scriptures used in divination.

Ogun – *Orisha* of iron and war who embodies the energies of aggression and protection. He rules the physical energy that moves our bodies. With his machete, he clears our path of obstacles. He's a warrior who lives in the forest. He's represented as a man on a horse with a gun or a machete and a loyal dog. His color is green. His offerings are hot chili peppers, cigars, rum and red palm oil. He was married to and divorced from Oshun. Ochosi is his brother.

Ogun La Kayay – Song declaring Ogun's eternal nature.

Olatunji – Nigerian drummer, Babatunde Olatunji, known for his groundbreaking 1959 album *Drums of Passion* and his collaborations with Carlos Santana and The Grateful Dead, among others. Died 2003.

Olokun – *Orisha* of the ocean, the masculine aspect of Yemoja associated with the dark, cold depths and raging storms. He's a scary merman with seaweed hair surrounded by dangerous fish hooks, torn nets and sunken ships. His color is navy blue. See Yemoja.

Oludumare – In Ifa, the energy of creation, perhaps equivalent to the Western idea of God, the intelligence above all, the spark of creation. Not a being but simply energy.

Ori – Yoruba word for head, mind or consciousness.

Orisha – An intermediary between humans and Oludumare, *Orishas* are actual historic persons who have ascended to divine status after their deaths in the distant past, like Catholic saints, but each *orisha* also embodies universal energy that is identified with a natural element. There are at least 400 *orishas* in the Ifa pantheon.

Orumilla – The original diviner who witnessed everything we've agreed to. Not an *orisha*, not a being. He's energy that knows each of us: what each individual stands for and against. Orunmilla is invoked at the beginning of every divination.

Oshun – *Orisha* of the river and fresh water who carries the energy of love and eroticism, personified as a beautiful woman. Her colors are yellow and gold. Her offerings are honey, yellow flowers, yellow candies, yellow fruit, mirrors and peacock feathers.

Oya – *Orisha* of the wind, the whirlwind, the tornado. She stands for truth, feminine leadership and feminine fury. Because she is our breath, she lives in the graveyard and helps people cross over at the time of death. She rules the changes in our lives. She is the sister of Oshun. She married and divorced Shango. Her colors are maroon, dark brown and deep purple. Eggplant is her favorite offering.

Pa ta – High notes of the *djembe* played with fingertips slapping the drumhead while the heel of the hand rests on the rim.

Rhumba – Drum rhythm invoking all 400 *orishas*.

Santeria – Indigenous Afro-Cuban religion based on Ifa.

Shango – *Orisha* of thunder, lightning and fire, expresses the energies of anger, judgment, justice, masculine leadership and manifestation. He was a king, and when he opens his mouth, he spits fire. He is the cleansing fire of healing that burns off all the irregularities of life. He's also a judge, so his symbol is the gavel. He's a warrior, and the double-headed ax is his weapon. Women are attracted to his sexual heat. His offerings are hot drinks, tobacco, chili peppers, red wine, whisky, alligator pepper and different kinds of kola nuts. His colors are red and white.

Smudge – To purify with fragrant smoke by burning the dried leaves of sacred herbs.

Sweatlodge – Native American healing ceremony where participants pray together in a dome-shaped tent heated by hot stones.

Umbanda – Indigenous religion of Brazil based on Ifa.

Vodou – Indigenous religion of Haiti with roots in several West Africa religions including Ifa.

Yankay – Ifa healing song translates as "cast it out."

Yemoja – *Orisha* of the ocean who expresses the energies of motherhood, prosperity and abundance. Yemoja is the feminine aspect who appears as the mermaid. She is the sparkle of sun or moonlight on the water. The frothy white foam is the train of her dress. Her colors are aqua blue, white and silver. She loves blue and white flowers, silver coins, wine and honey, but Yemoja's favorite offering is watermelon, for the sweetness of the water.

Yoruba – One of the largest ethnic groups in West Africa, estimated at 30 to 50 million people. Their origins may go back to the 4th century BC. Their culture thrived in what is now western Nigeria between 1100 and 1900 AD and was known for fine bronze sculpture, pottery, textiles and music.

Zendo – A room dedicated to Zen Buddhist meditation.

About the author

Marsha Scarbrough is the author *of Medicine Dance: One woman's healing journey into the world of Native American sweatlodges, drumming meditations and dance fasts.* As a freelance journalist, she has had over 75 articles published in national magazines, including *Inside "Breaking Bad,"* now available as a Kindle eBook. As an Assistant Director, she spent 17 years in Hollywood scheduling, planning and running the sets of feature films and prime time television. Marsha has traveled with Buddhist teacher Joan Halifax, danced with movement guru Gabrielle Roth, earned a brown belt in karate from martial arts legend Tak Kubota, participated in Native American healing ceremonies and produced African drumming workshops. In 2006, Marsha moved from her native Los Angeles to Santa Fe, New Mexico. Since 2010, Marsha has spent her summers teaching English to speakers of other languages at Santa Fe University of Art and Design. She spends winter traveling the world. For more about Marsha, visit her website www.marshascarbrough.com.

CHANGE
MAKERS
BOOKS

Changemakers publishes books for individuals committed to transforming their lives and transforming the world. Our readers seek to become positive, powerful agents of change. Changemakers books inform, inspire, and provide practical wisdom and skills to empower us to create the next chapter of humanity's future.
Please visit our website at www.changemakers-books.com